Knitting the Perfect Pair

Knitting the Perfect Pair

Secrets to Great Socks

Dorothy T. Ratigan

cincinnati, ohio
www.mycraftivity.com
connect. create. explore.

Other fine books from Krause Publications are available from your local bookstore, craft store or visit us at our Web site at www.fwmedia.com.

13 12 11 10 09   5 4 3 2 1

Distributed in Canada by Fraser Direct
100 Armstrong Avenue
Georgetown, ON, Canada L7G 5S4
Tel: (905) 877-4411

Distributed in the U.K. and Europe by David & Charles
Brunel House, Newton Abbot, Devon, TQ12 4PU, England
Tel: (+44) 1626 323200, Fax: (+44) 1626 323319
E-mail: postmaster@davidandcharles.co.uk

Distributed in Australia by Capricorn Link
P.O. Box 704, S. Windsor NSW, 2756 Australia
Tel: (02) 4577-3555

Library of Congress Cataloging in Publication Data
Ratigan, Dorothy T.
 Knitting the perfect pair : secrets to great socks
/ Dorothy T. Ratigan. -- 1st ed.
   p. cm.
 Includes bibliographical references and index.
 ISBN 978-1-60061-052-3 (alk. paper)
 1. Knitting--Patterns. 2. Socks. I. Title.
 TT825.R332 2009
 746.43'2041--dc22
                              2008053902

Editor: Jennifer Claydon
Designer: Rachael Smith
Production Coordinator: Matt Wagner
Photographer: Ric Deliantoni
Stylist: Lauren Emmerling
Illustrators: Toni Toomey and Kara Gott
Technical Editor: Alexandra Virgiel

Metric Conversion Chart

To convert	to	multiply by
Inches	Centimeters	2.54
Centimeters	Inches	0.4
Feet	Centimeters	30.5
Centimeters	Feet	0.03
Yards	Meters	0.9
Meters	Yards	1.1

About the Author

Dorothy T. Ratigan's career in fiber arts spans thirty years. As a shop owner, she sold needlecraft supplies and taught classes in knitting, crewelwork, crochet, needlepoint, bargello, embroidery, cross-stitch and weaving. As president and co-owner of Pine Tree Knitters, she designed knitted skiwear, oversaw a production staff and marketed finished items to L.L.Bean, Eddie Bauer and others. As a designer and technical editor, she has worked for Brown Sheep Company, Inc.; North Island Designs; *Knitting World* magazine; *Knitter's* magazine; *Interweave Knits* magazine; and *PieceWork* magazine. Dorothy has also worked on countless books, including the One-Skein Wonders series (Storey Publishing, LLC), the Bond Collection and many Interweave Press titles. One of her designs is featured in *Vogue Knitting: The Ultimate Knitting Book* (Sixth&Spring Books).

Dedication

This book is dedicated with love to Mike, Steve and Austin for sharing their love, humor and patience.

Acknowledgments

My adventure with needlework began with the skills that my mother, Peg, and her sisters, Nell and Delia, brought from Ireland and passed on to me; I am grateful for my good fortune.

My family and friends provided prayers, support and comments, solicited and unsolicited, constructive and otherwise, which helped to put things in perspective.

Thanks to Jay Staten and Jennifer Claydon at F+W Media for their optimism, indispensable assistance and for keeping me focused.

Without the knitting help of Judy Warde and Don Bean, who stepped up to the plate when things went south, I'd still be working on this book. And I'm grateful to Charlotte Tanson for always having the time to look and listen.

Special thanks go out to my friend and wordsmith Judith Durant who is always only a phone call away, even when we're on separate continents. She is invaluable to my success.

Last, but not least, my heartfelt thanks go to Bob for being there daily with laughter and encouragement to keep my spirits soaring.

Introduction

Knitting has been a part of my life for so long that it's hard to remember when the adventure began. Like most knitters, my lessons began with learning to knit and purl and evolved into using those two stitches to create a variety of textures and designs in knitted fabric. Very early on, the technical aspects of knitting fascinated me, and my time was spent discovering things like how one simple flip of the wrist can affect the outcome of a project. Whenever knitting instructions said something like, "Be careful not to twist the stitches," I would cast on and deliberately twist the stitches just to see what happened. In addition to learning why not to do certain things, these exercises uncovered ways of putting some of these "don'ts" to good use.

While planning a book on sock knitting, my mind was flooded with thoughts of various cast ons and bind offs, of multidirectional and multicolor knitting, of different styles of heels, soles and toes. Being limited to a dozen sock designs, my goal was to vary the styles and offer as many techniques as possible. There are knee-highs, ankle socks and everything in between, and of course you'll find various heel turnings and toe shapings. One sock even has a leg worked in a different direction from the foot! If you're a knitter who follows patterns word-by-word, you'll find specific instructions and plenty of variety, with a sock style for everyone on your list. If you like to pick up features to mix and match with others, I hope you learn a few new tricks and techniques to add to your collection.

Enjoy the adventure, keep good notes and share what you learn!

A Brief History of Knitted Socks

The history of hand-knitted socks seems to begin in thirteenth-century Islamic Egypt, and fragments of these early blue and white stockings, knitted in cotton, can be found in several museum collections. However, in Western costume, socks and stockings were most commonly made from cloth cut on the bias until around 1590 when knitted stockings, often made from silk, replaced them. Worn by men with their breeches, stockings were knitted in bright colors such as yellow and adorned with colored silk, and sometimes gold, thread. Knitted socks and stockings, made by hand and by machine, have been a part of our wardrobe ever since.

During the eighteenth century, white stockings for men in the upper classes were *de rigueur*, and when women began showing a little ankle in the late part of that century, stockings became decorative, being ribbed or embroidered. At the turn of the century and into the early nineteenth century, men's stockings could be white, colored, striped, plain or fancy knit. Throughout most of the nineteenth century, stockings for women were rarely seen and were generally black, knitted in cotton or wool for daywear and in silk for the evening.

Changes in sock style began in the early twentieth century. Men began wearing black silk socks for evening, and casual socks were patterned, striped or spotted. Argyle became the rage during the 1920s, and these and other patterned socks were sported by men with their plus fours or knickerbockers, both on and off the golf course. Nylon was developed during the 1930s and women largely abandoned other styles of socks in favor of the new "artificial silk" stockings. When pants became the wardrobe piece of choice for many women, garter belts and stockings once again made way for knitted socks.

In recent American history, hand knitting socks has become a craze of enormous proportions. In her book *Folk Socks*, Nancy Bush reports that an article written by Joan Thirsk estimated that during the sixteenth century, somewhere between nine and eleven million pairs of socks were knitted per year in the United Kingdom. While American knitters may not be quite that prolific, a search for knitted sock patterns on the Internet returns hundreds of thousands of results, and a search on sock yarn turns up even more links! Walk into any yarn shop and you'll find a whole section devoted to sock yarn. It is available in wool, acrylic, silk, bamboo and wool blended with everything from cashmere to soy. Ankle, calf or knee length; one-, two-, or multicolored; cabled, ribbed or lacy; if you can imagine them, you can knit them.

If you'd like to research knitting further, see the *Bibliography* on page 109; several fine books for answers to questions you may encounter in your pursuit of knitting perfection can be found there.

Chapter One

Materials and Tools

Today's knitters are crazy about socks, and the knitting industry supports this craze by producing a seemingly endless variety of yarns, needles and tools to knit them. So how do you choose? The following pages give some guidelines for selecting an appropriate yarn for your chosen pattern and the best needles for your chosen yarn and design. You'll also find a list of other handy tools to support your sock-knitting habit.

Yarn Selection

The yarns used in this book were chosen for the particular type and style of sock they were to become. There are hundreds of sock yarns available to today's knitter, and they vary in fiber content, weight and look. There is no better way to determine the best yarn for a particular project than by swatching. You can either choose a yarn you love, do a couple of swatches and then select the right sock style for it, or work in the reverse—choose a sock pattern and use the suggested yarn, or use the suggested yarn as a guide to pick one that is more to your liking. In either case, the swatch is of utmost importance, allowing you to determine gauge, density, elasticity and pattern definition.

Yarn Content

Each pattern in Chapter Three specifies the fiber content of the yarn used for the modeled socks. Sock yarn can be made up of fibers that are blended or pure, natural or synthetic. Among the many varieties used in this book, you'll find superwash wool blended with nylon; superwash wool blended with microfiber and cashmere; superwash wool blended with nylon and mohair; bamboo blended with wool and nylon; llama blended with wool; and many more. You'll also find 100 percent wool as well as 100 percent superwash wool.

When selecting yarn, it's important to keep in mind the recipient of your labor of love. If the socks will be hand washed, you may choose from any of the 100 percent natural animal fibers. If the socks will be thrown into a washing machine, your best bet is to choose a blended, washable fiber. One of my favorites is a combination of superwash wool, mohair and nylon. It provides warmth, softness and strength.

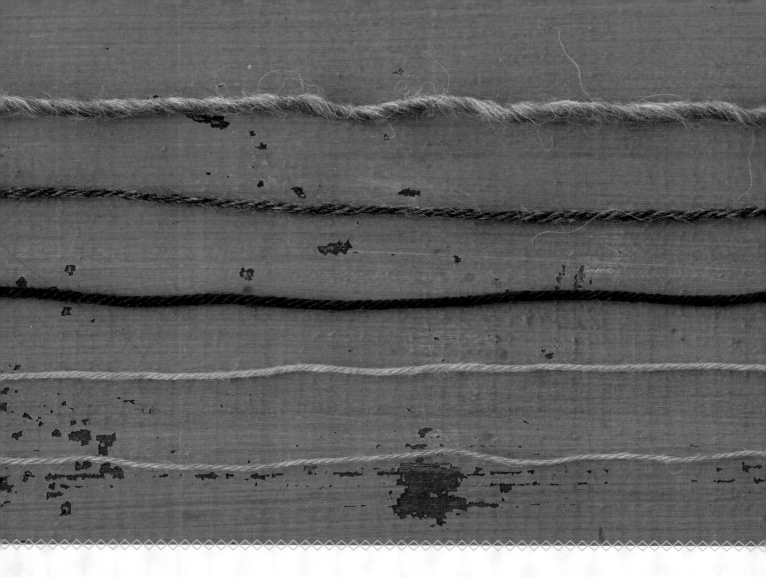

Yarn Weight

The weight of the yarn chosen is also listed with each set of instructions. To learn more about yarn weights, see the *Yarn Weight Guidelines* on page 107. Yarn weights used in this book vary from fingering to sport to DK to worsted to heavy worsted. Heavy worsted weight yarn can be used for slippers or indoor socks—it's too thick to wear with shoes or boots. Worsted weight yarns work best for boot socks, where there's plenty of room for the bulk. Worsted weight yarn is also more rugged than some of the lighter yarns and will stand up to heavy wear. Any of the other yarn weights, from DK to lace, can be used for socks. Again, the best way to choose the right yarn for your socks is by doing a swatch at the gauge specified in the pattern, making sure you like the feel of the resulting fabric.

Yarn Color and Texture

Finally, it's important that you get yarn with the right look for your socks. Yarn is available in an abundance of solid colors, heathered colors, variegated hand-painted varieties and even self-patterning designs. Yarns can also be smooth or textured. In general, smooth yarns work best for socks—you don't want to feel nubs of bouclé under your feet. However, you could choose a textured yarn for the leg and a smooth one in a coordinating color for the foot. Just be sure that you like the combination of your chosen yarns with the pattern. It would be disappointing to spend the time doing an elaborate, lacy pattern only to see that it is obscured by the shifting colors of a variegated yarn. Once again, you can make the best choice through swatching.

Needle Selection

There's a movement afoot (pun intended) among certain sock knitters to let double-pointed needles become extinct. Sock designers have published instructions for knitting socks with two circular needles, with one circular needle, and even for knitting two socks at once with one long circular needle. No slight intended to these ideas, but I prefer double-pointed needles, in either longer 8"–10" (20cm–25cm) lengths or shorter 4"–6" (10cm–15cm) lengths.

Some double-pointed needles come in sets of four, some in sets of five. Depending on the stitch used, pattern or knitter's preference, the stitches may be divided onto either three or four needles with the fourth or fifth needle working the stitches. Although most of the patterns in this book are worked on five needles, at times the stitch multiple of a pattern, such as in the *Traveling Stitch Socks* on page 72, lends itself to four needles.

Needles come in a variety of materials, including various types of wood, bamboo, plastic and metal. Choosing one over the other is largely a matter of what feels best in your hands, but this choice can also be dependent on the fiber you're using. In general, wooden needles add a slight bit of friction to the knitting, so the stitches are less likely to inadvertently slip off the needles. This can be an advantage for the beginner or for any knitter working with a particularly slippery yarn. Metal needles are slick, allowing for smoother knitting of coarser fibers such as wool and mohair, as well as really speedy knitting with those slippery yarns. There is no right or wrong choice here—four or five, long or short, wood or metal—it's really a matter of personal preference.

Other Sock-Knitting Tools

1. Needle Holders

To keep my double-pointed needles together and orderly when not in use, I use elastic eyeglass holders. The center coil can be moved from side to side, making one loop larger or smaller, so they will accommodate a set of five needles up to US 7 (4.5mm). You can tag the second loop with the needle size. The elastic used in the loops won't leave any residue on the needles and won't dry out like rubber bands do.

2. Point Protectors

When traveling, I always put point protectors on both ends of all needles to ensure that the stitches are all in place when I arrive at my destination.

I also use them on the needles holding instep stitches while working a heel—this is protection against inadvertently letting them drop off the needle while concentrating on the heel.

3. Thread Cutter

This is an invaluable aid to any knitter, especially a traveling one, since scissors are no longer allowed on airplanes. Most cutters are made with a hole at the top so that it can be strung onto a leather cord, beaded chain or ribbon and worn around the neck for convenience.

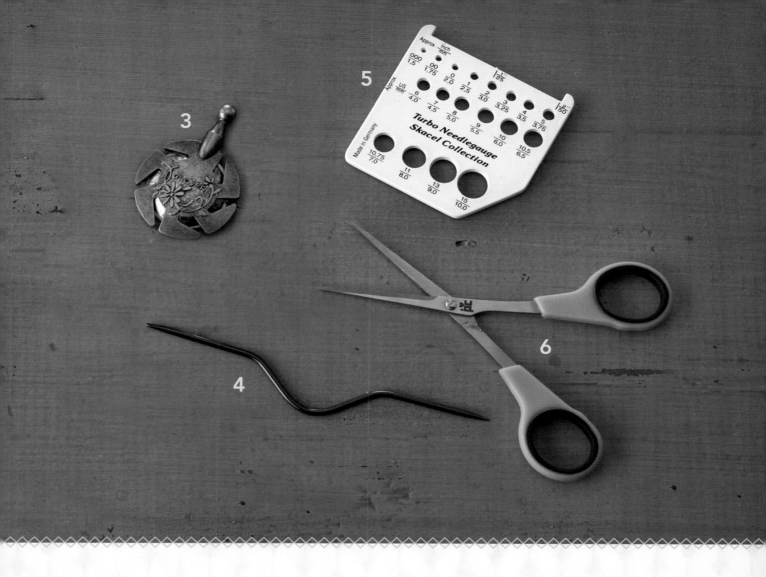

4. Cable Needle

Cable needles are used to temporarily hold stitches while a cable is formed in knitting. To make a cable, stitches are worked in a different order than normal, which creates a twist within the fabric. Cable needles come in several different shapes; I prefer to use a U-shaped cable needle.

5. Needle Gauge

This handy tool will tell you what size your needles are, which is especially important for double-pointed needles since many of them don't have a size printed on them. You may notice that needles sold as the same size but produced by different companies are not, in fact, the same size. I suggest that you find sock needles that you like and buy different sets of that same brand; this way your gauge should remain consistent from project to project.

6. Scissors

Enough can't be said about a quality pair of sharp scissors that is sized for your project. Use your scissors for fiber arts only; never cut string or paper with your good scissors or they'll quickly become dull.

Chapter Two
Techniques

There are many ways to cast on for knitting, and some are more appropriate for one purpose than another. This chapter shows several different cast-on methods and highlights the advantages of each. And that's just the beginning: You'll also find heel variations, toe variations, as well as basic information about knitting, purling, increasing, decreasing and grafting. Tips for caring for hand-knitted socks are also included.

Directional Knitting

The two most common ways to knit socks are from the cuff down to the toe or from the toe up to the cuff. There are other methods to follow (see the *Sea Squall Socks* on page 62), but these two methods should serve you well through most of your sock-knitting adventures.

Cuff Down

Most sock patterns are worked from the cuff down to the toe, and in my opinion this is the easiest method. The only downside that I can see is that when stitch patterns are used, they will appear upside down.

Toe Up

Working from the toe up to the cuff can be more challenging than working from the cuff down. One advantage to working from the toe up is that you can place the stitches on a holder and try the sock on before turning the heel for a perfect fit.

Leg and Foot Measurements

There is nothing like wearing a sock that was made to your own specific measurements, so for that perfect fit take the following measurements before you begin knitting. First, determine where on your leg you'd like the cuff to rest. There are standard sock sizes, such as knee-highs or ankle socks, or you can choose a length anywhere in between. Measure from where you'd like the cuff to rest to the top of the heel. This is the leg length. Next, measure the circumference of the foot at its widest point—on most people, this will be at the ball of the foot. This measurement will be the circumference of the leg and the foot of the sock. Most patterns will say, "continue until foot measures 2" (5cm) from desired finished length." Measure the length of the foot from the back of the heel to the end of the toe. Subtract the 2" (5cm) from this measurement to find foot length. The toe length measurement used for most sock patterns is 2" (5cm).

Standard Sizes

If you don't know the exact measurements of the foot you are knitting for, here are some general guidelines you can follow.

	Leg/foot circumference	Foot length
Children	5"–6½" (13cm–17cm)	3"–6" (8cm–15cm)
Women	7"–8" (18cm–20cm)	8"–11" (20cm–28cm)
Men	8"–9" (20cm–23cm)	9"–12" (23cm–30cm)

Casting On for Cuff-Down Socks

There are a variety of cast ons available to the sock knitter. A major consideration is flexibility—keeping cast-on stitches as elastic as possible adds to the comfort and wearability of the sock. The other consideration is appearance, and you'll be surprised at how different the various cast ons appear. I suggest casting on with a needle that is a size or two larger than the needles you'll be knitting with, then transferring the stitches to the correct needles. This method keeps the cast on elastic and prevents loose stitches from forming between the needles. Following are the cast-on techniques used in the patterns in this book.

Long-Tail Cast On

This method creates a knit stitch and is the most commonly used cast on for sock knitting.

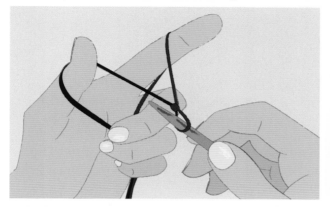

1. Position yarn

Make a slip knot, leaving a long tail (at least 4" [10cm] for every 1" [3cm] you'll be casting on). Slide the slip knot onto the needle with the long tail toward the back of the needle. Slide your thumb and index finger between the 2 strands of yarn. Wrap the long tail around your index finger and the strand still attached to the skein around your thumb. Grasp both strands with your remaining fingers.

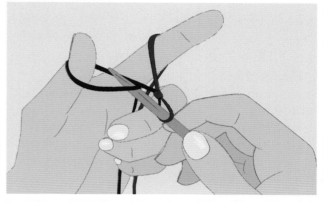

2. Bring needle through front loop

Slide the tip of the needle up through the loop of yarn wrapped around your thumb from front to back.

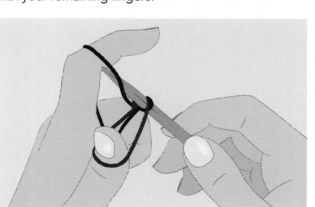

3. Catch second strand

Keeping the needle in the loop of yarn around the thumb, hook the needle behind the strand of yarn on the front of your index finger.

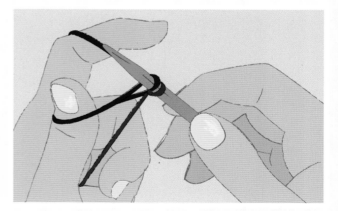

4. Draw back strand through front loop

Bring the yarn through the loop of yarn on your thumb, creating a second loop on your needle (the first cast-on stitch). Drop the loop of yarn on your thumb. Gently tug on the strands to tighten the cast-on stitch. Repeat to cast on the remaining stitches. Include the slip knot in your stitch count.

Long-Tail Cast On Variation

This method works in the same manner as the Long-Tail Cast On, but creates a purl stitch.

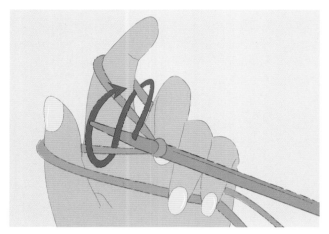

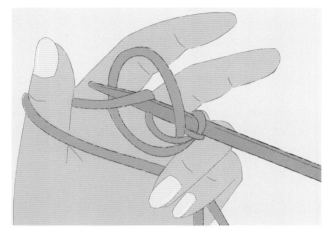

1. Begin stitch

Position yarn as described in Step 1 of Long-Tail Cast On (see page 25). Slide the tip of the needle through the loop of yarn wrapped around your index finger from back to front. Keeping the needle in the loop of yarn around the index finger, hook the strand of yarn on the back of your thumb.

2. Complete stitch

Bring the yarn through the loop of yarn on your index finger, creating a new loop on your needle. Drop the loop on your index finger and gently tug on the strands to tighten the cast-on stitch. Repeat to cast on the remaining stitches. Include the slip knot in your stitch count.

Rolled Edge Cast On

This cast on creates a very elastic cuff and begins with half the total number of stitches needed for the leg of the sock.

Using waste yarn, cast on the amount of stitches needed onto a straight needle and knit 2 rows. Divide the stitches onto 4 double-pointed needles, join for working in the round and continue to knit with waste yarn for 2 rounds. With a smooth cotton or nylon ravel cord, knit 1 round.

ROUND 1: Join the main sock yarn, *knit 1, yarn over; repeat from * to end of round.

ROUND 2: *Knit 1, yarn forward, slip 1 purlwise, yarn back; repeat from * to end of round.

ROUND 3: *Yarn back, slip 1 purlwise, yarn forward, purl 1; repeat from * to end of round.

ROUND 4: *Knit 1, purl 1; repeat from * to end of round.

Change to the needle that will be used to knit the rib. Continue in the rib pattern for the desired length. Remove the ravel cord by pulling on one end of it. The waste yarn will separate from the main yarn leaving an elastic cuff.

If you choose to work a K2, P2 rib, the number of stitches cast on must be divisible by four. Separate the knit and purl stitches onto separate needles. With the needle that will be used to knit the rib, work 2 knit stitches followed by 2 purl stitches over all stitches.

Patterned Cast On

If a sock cuff begins with a pattern such as ribbing or seed stitch, a Patterned Cast On lends a crisp look to the top of the sock. This method provides an elastic cast on that easily springs back into shape.

Follow the pattern of the sock to determine the number of stitches to cast on as knit stitches using the Long-Tail Cast On (see page 25) and the number of purl stitches to cast on using the Long-Tail Cast On Variation (see page 26). For example, if the sock begins with a K2, P2 rib, cast on 2 stitches using the Long-Tail Cast On, then 2 stitches using the Long-Tail Cast On Variation. Continue to cast on by alternating 2 knit cast-on stitches and 2 purl cast-on stitches until the correct number of stitches have been cast on.

Two-Needle Long-Tail Cast On

Use this method to prevent the cast-on edge from being too tight and rolling upwards. This is especially important when knitting socks with lace patterns. Simply work the Long-Tail Cast On (see page 25) over 2 needles, or cast on with a needle that is 3 sizes larger than the ones you'll knit with.

Two-Color Braided Cast On

This is a decorative cast on that looks great at the top of any sock, but especially multicolored socks. The cast on is done with 2 colors; alternating the 2 colors over 2 rows forms the braid.

Holding 2 yarns together (Color A and Color B), form a slip knot and place it on the needle. Cast on an even number of stitches using the Long-Tail Cast On (see page 25) with Color A over the thumb and Color B over the index finger. Distribute the stitches evenly onto 4 double-pointed needles. Drop the slip stitch and join into a round, taking care not to twist the stitches. Knit one round with Color A.

NEXT ROUND: With both yarns forward, *purl 1 B, drop B, bring A over B, purl 1 A, drop A, bring B over A; rep from * to end of round.

NEXT ROUND: With both yarns forward, *purl 1 B, drop B, bring A under B, purl 1 A, drop A, bring B under A; rep from * to end of round.

Provisional Crochet Cast On

This is the cast on to use if you want to knit the leg of a sock back and forth and join it with Kitchener stitch to form a tube. See the *Sea Squall Socks* on page 62 for an example of this type of construction.

1. Set up for cast on

With waste yarn and a crochet hook, chain 5. Hold a knitting needle and the crochet hook parallel (with the crochet hook on right). Bring the waste yarn under the knitting needle.

2. Wrap yarn

Bring the crochet hook over the knitting needle and wrap the yarn around the crochet hook.

3. Form loop

Draw the yarn through the loop on the hook to form the first cast-on stitch on the knitting needle.

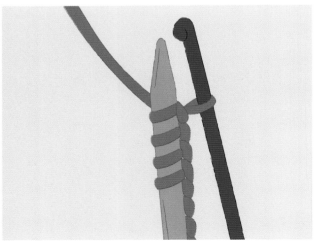

4. Continue casting on

Repeat Steps 1–3 (omitting the chain 5 at the beginning of Step 1) to cast on the number of stitches indicated in the pattern.

Invisible Provisional Cast On

With this cast on, plain or ribbed stitches remain live so they can be folded down and knit together with leg stitches, forming a doubled cuff. This can be used to add stability to the top of a calf-length sock or for the top of a short sport sock that won't slip down into your shoe.

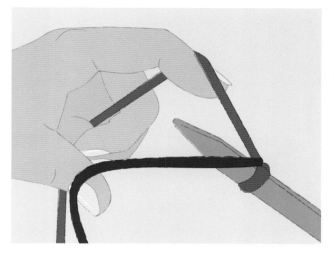

1. Set up for cast on
Holding sock yarn and waste yarn together, make a slip knot and place it on the needle. With the sock yarn over your index finger and the waste yarn over your thumb, bring the needle under the waste yarn from front to back.

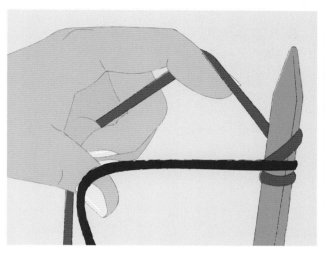

2. Continue first stitch
Bring the needle over the top of the sock yarn.

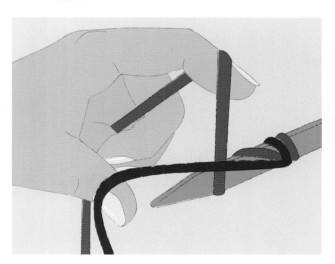

3. Complete first stitch
Bring the needle under the waste yarn from back to front, completing the first stitch.

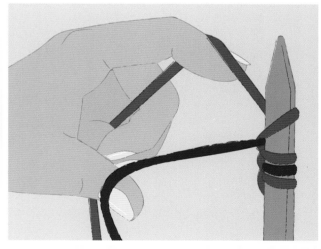

4. Continue casting on
Bring the needle over the sock yarn, placing a second stitch on the needle. Continue casting on until you have the number of stitches indicated in the pattern.

When the cuff is complete, insert a circular needle into the live cast-on stitches and remove the waste yarn. Bring the circular needle in back of the live stitches on the double-pointed needles and knit 1 stitch from each needle together.

Casting On for Toe-Up Socks

Casting on for a pair of toe-up socks is very different from casting on for cuff-down socks because the toe of the sock must be closed at the beginning of the knitting rather than at the end. Here is one method for starting socks from the toe up.

Crochet Circular Cast On
This method makes a neat toe with no bulk.

1. Begin cast on
Leaving a 4" (10cm) tail to be woven in later, wrap the yarn twice loosely around your thumb. Remove the loop from your thumb. Work 8 single crochets into the loop, leaving the stitches on the crochet hook.

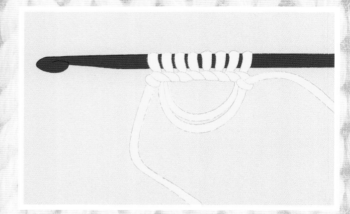

2. Distribute stitches
Distribute the stitches onto 4 double-pointed needles, 2 stitches on each needle.

3. Close circle
Pull on the tail to snug up the stitches into a tight ring.

Joining in a Round

◇◇◇◇◇◇◇◇◇◇◇◇◇◇◇◇◇◇◇◇◇◇◇◇◇◇◇◇◇◇◇◇

For most sock patterns, once you've cast on, you'll join stitches to work in the round. Put a little work into learning this technique and you will be rewarded for the rest of your knitting life!

1. Cast on stitches
Cast on the required number of stitches onto 1 needle.

2. Distribute stitches
Divide the cast-on stitches as evenly as possible among a set of double-pointed needles. If you are using a set of 4 double-pointed needles, distribute the stitches over 3 needles, leaving 1 needle for working. If you are using a set of 5 double-pointed needles, distribute the stitches over 4 needles, leaving 1 needle for working. When dividing the stitches, slip the stitches onto the new needle as if to purl, otherwise your cast-on row will have twisted stitches. Lay the needles down on a flat surface with the working yarn on the right. Carefully straighten the cast-on row so that the bottom of each stitch is toward the inside of the needles and none of the stitches are twisted around the needles.

3. Join stitches
Hold the needle with the working yarn in your right hand and the needle with the first cast-on stitch in your left hand. Insert the tip of the free needle into the first cast-on stitch. Wrap the working yarn around the tip of the free needle and knit the first stitch.

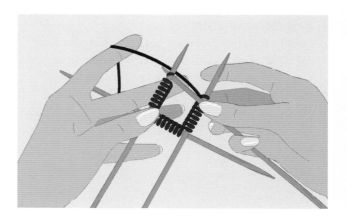

Basic Stitches

◇◇◇

After casting on and joining, it's time to knit! If you can easily interpret diagrams and written instructions, the following pages should set you on your course. If not, there are many other avenues to look to for guidance and information, such as classes at your local yarn shop, knitting guild or group, knitting programs on television and DVD or instructional downloads from the Internet.

The Knit Stitch

Follow these steps to form a knit stitch.

1. Position needles

With the working yarn wrapped over your left index finger, insert the right-hand needle into the first stitch on the left-hand needle from front to back. The right-hand needle should cross behind the left-hand needle.

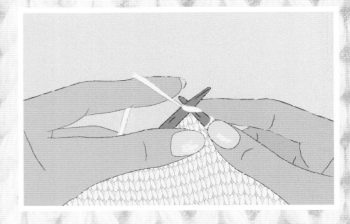

2. Wrap yarn

Bring the right-hand needle tip behind the yarn in front of your left index finger. The working yarn should be wrapped around the tip of the right-hand needle counterclockwise.

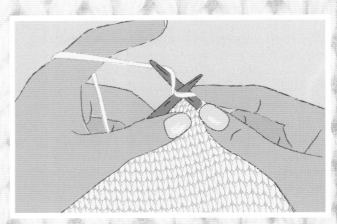

3. Create new stitch

Dip the needle tip down and pull the wrapped yarn through the stitch on the left-hand needle. Bring the yarn up on the right-hand needle to create a new stitch, allowing the old stitch to slide easily off the left-hand needle. The new stitch remains on the right-hand needle.

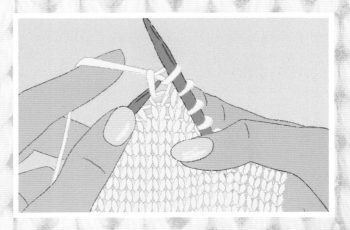

The Purl Stitch

Follow these steps to form a purl stitch.

1. Position needles

With the working yarn in your left hand, slide the tip of the right-hand needle into the first stitch on the left-hand needle from back to front. The right-hand needle should cross in front of the left-hand needle.

For illustration purposes, the working yarn is shown held between the index finger and thumb. However, when working a row of purl stitches, the yarn should remain in the position shown in Step 2 to create proper tension.

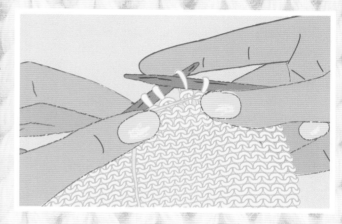

2. Wrap yarn

Use your left hand to wrap the working yarn around the tip of the right-hand needle counterclockwise. Draw the right-hand needle back through the stitch on the left-hand needle, catching the wrapped working yarn with the tip of the needle. Bring the working yarn through the stitch on the left-hand needle.

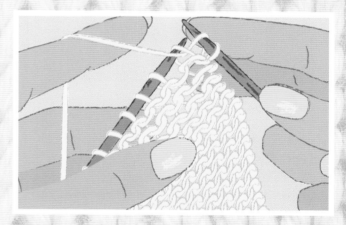

3. Create new stitch

Bring the yarn up on the right-hand needle to create a new stitch, allowing the old stitch to slide off the left-hand needle. The new stitch remains on the right-hand needle.

For illustration purposes, the working yarn is shown held between the index finger and thumb. However, when working a row of purl stitches, the yarn should remain in the position shown in Step 2 to create proper tension.

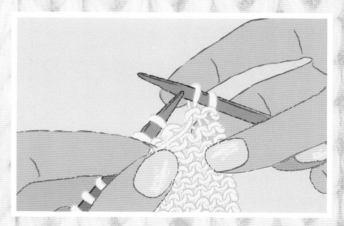

Decreases and Increases

◇◇◇◇◇◇◇◇◇◇◇◇◇◇◇◇◇◇◇◇◇◇◇◇◇◇◇◇◇◇◇◇◇◇◇◇

Decreasing and increasing allow you to shape your knitting to any size. Eliminating stitches makes the piece smaller, and adding stitches makes the piece larger. Once you've familiarized yourself with these basic shaping techniques, you're ready to shape any of the patterns in the book.

Knit Two Together (k2tog)

This technique really is as simple as it sounds. By placing the tip of the needle through 2 stitches instead of 1, you knit the stitches together into a single stitch.

Slide the right-hand needle into 2 stitches together from front to back, as for a regular knit stitch. Knit the 2 stitches together as 1 stitch. This will lower your stitch count by 1 stitch. When the 2 stitches have been knitted together, you will see that the decrease leans to the right.

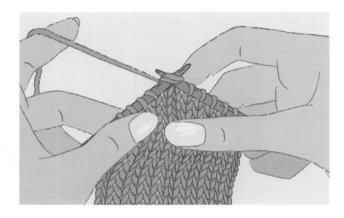

Slip One, Knit One, Pass Slipped Stitch Over (SKP)

This technique is also fairly self-explanatory. By passing an unworked stitch over a worked stitch, you reduce the number of stitches.

Slip 1 stitch from the left-hand needle to the right-hand needle. Knit the stitch at the end of the left-hand needle. Insert the left-hand needle into the second stitch from the tip of the right-hand needle. Pull that stitch over the first stitch at the end of the right-hand needle and off of the needle. This will lower your stitch count by 1 stitch. This decrease leans to the left.

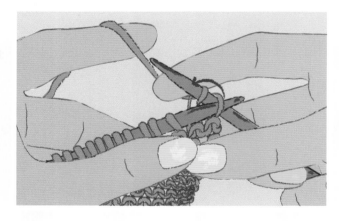

Slip, Slip, Knit (SSK)

The SSK is the left-leaning symmetrical sister of k2tog that brings perfect symmetry to your knitted piece.

1. Slip stitches

Insert the tip of the right-hand needle into the first stitch on the left-hand needle as if to knit. Slip the stitch off of the left-hand needle onto the right-hand needle. Repeat with a second stitch.

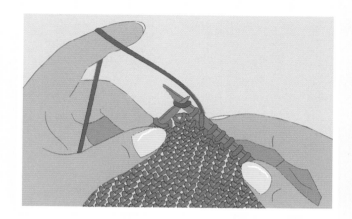

2. Position needles

Insert the left-hand needle into the fronts of both slipped stitches. The left-hand needle should cross in front of the right-hand needle. Wrap the working yarn around the right-hand needle, counterclockwise.

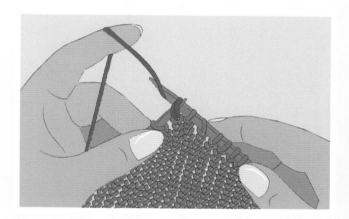

3. Knit stitches together

Knit the 2 stitches together as 1 stitch. This will lower your stitch count by 1 stitch. When the 2 stitches have been knitted together, you will see that the decrease leans to the left.

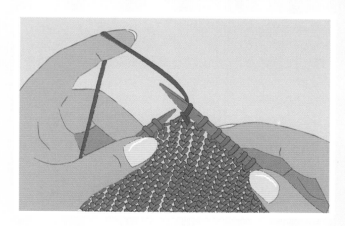

Knit One Front and Back (KFB)

The title of this technique explains the process very clearly. By knitting a single stitch twice, you create two stitches where there used to be one.

1. Knit into front of stitch
Slip the right-hand needle into the first stitch on the left-hand needle from front to back and knit the stitch as usual, but do not slip the stitch off the left-hand needle yet.

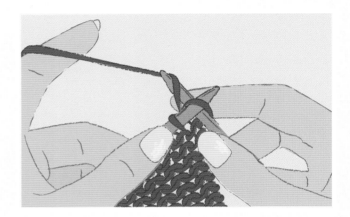

2. Knit into back of stitch
Insert the right-hand needle through the back of the same stitch and knit another stitch.

3. Create new stitch
Slide the old stitch off the left-hand needle. The right-hand needle now has 2 new stitches. This will increase your stitch count by 1 stitch.

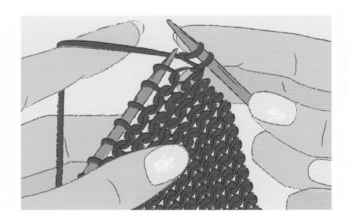

Closing the Toe

◇◇◇◇◇◇◇◇◇◇◇◇◇◇◇◇◇◇◇◇◇◇◇◇◇◇◇◇◇◇◇

There are two main techniques that can be used to close the toe of a sock. Follow the pattern's instructions to choose a technique.

Drawing Up

This technique is used to tie off a few stitches left at the end of a pattern.

1. Slip stitches

After working the last round of the pattern, cut the working yarn, leaving at least a 10" (25cm) tail. Thread the yarn tail through the eye of a tapestry needle. Slip all of the stitches from the knitting needles to the tapestry needle.

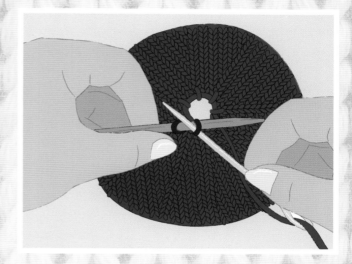

2. Tighten stitches

Pull the yarn tail through the stitches. Pull on the yarn tail, tightening the stitches until there is no gap at the closing point. Insert the tapestry needle into the center of the tightened stitches and pull the yarn tail through to the inside of the knitting. Weave the yarn tail into the wrong side of the knitting to secure it.

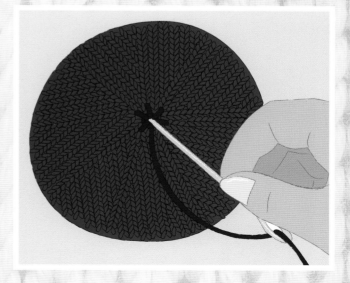

Kitchener Stitch

Use Kitchener stitch any time you need to join two rows of live stitches together. Kitchener stitch, when done correctly, looks like just another row of knitting and is as perfectly elastic as your knitted fabric.

1. Make first set-up stitch

Transfer the stitches to be seamed evenly onto 2 needles. Make sure the working yarn is at the end of the needle. Thread a tapestry needle with yarn. Hold the needles together in your left hand with the wrong sides facing inward and the right sides facing outward . Insert the threaded tapestry needle into the first stitch on the front needle as if to purl. Pull the tapestry needle through the stitch, leaving the stitch on the needle.

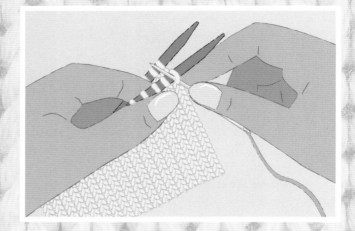

2. Make second set-up stitch

Insert the tapestry needle into the first stitch on the back needle as if to knit. Pull the tapestry needle through the stitch, leaving the stitch on the needle.

Steps 1 and 2 are only done to set up for seaming. Once these preparatory stitches are complete, the rest of the stitches will be seamed in the following pattern: knit, purl, purl, knit.

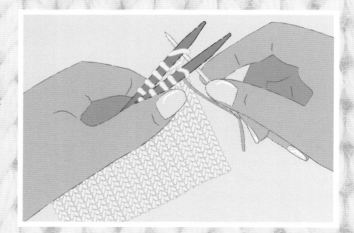

3. Slip stitch from front needle

Insert the tapestry needle into the first stitch on the front needle again, this time as if to knit, and slip it off the end of the needle.

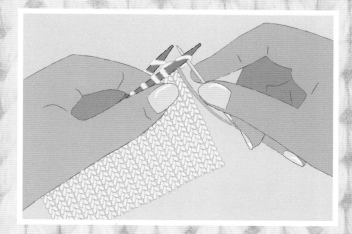

4. Continue grafting

Insert the tapestry needle into the next stitch on the front needle as if to purl. Pull the tapestry needle through the stitch, leaving the stitch on the needle. Pull the yarn through the stitch, but do not excessively tighten the seam.

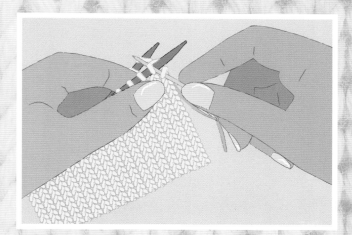

5. Slip stitch from back needle

Insert the tapestry needle into the first stitch on the back needle again, this time as if to purl, and slip it off the end of the needle.

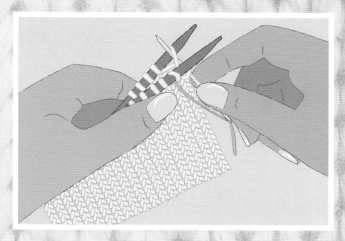

6. Continue grafting

Insert the threaded tapestry needle into the next stitch on the back needle as if to knit. Pull the tapestry needle through the stitch, leaving the stitch on the needle. Pull the yarn through the stitch, but do not excessively tighten the seam.

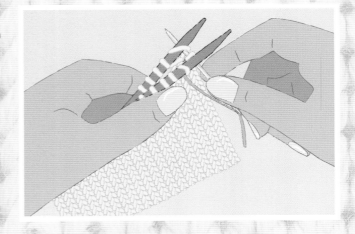

7. Finish grafting

Repeat Steps 3–6 until all of the stitches are grafted together. The seaming yarn will appear loosely woven between the 2 rows of grafted stitches.

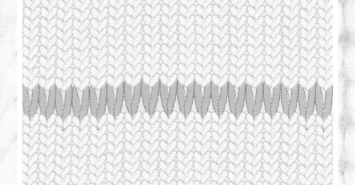

8. Adjust tension of seaming yarn

If you have not been adjusting the tension of the stitches as you grafted, gently adjust the tension of the seaming yarn until it matches the tension of the knitted fabric. When the seaming yarn is properly tensioned, the seam should be invisible.

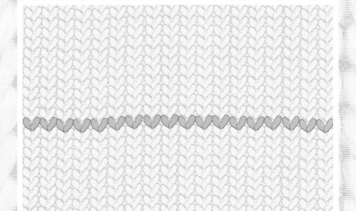

Binding Off a Cuff

This technique can be used to bind off the cuff of a toe-up sock.

Tapestry Needle Bind Off

You'll need this type of bind off when working a sock from the toe up. It produces an edge similar to the Rolled Edge Cast On (see page 26). It is elastic and bounces back into shape when relaxed. The easiest way of working this stitch is to place the knit and the purl stitches onto separate needles held parallel to each other.

Wrap the yarn around the sock top 3½ times to measure the length required for the bind off. Break the yarn and thread the tail through a tapestry needle. Separate the knit and purl stitches on Needle 1 onto 2 needles, holding the knit stitches in front of the purl stitches. Slip the last purl stitch from Needle 4 to Needle 1.

With the yarn forward, pass the tapestry needle through the first knit stitch on the front needle from back to front, then through the first purl stitch on the back needle from front to back. *Bring the yarn forward and pass through the first stitch on the knit needle from front to back, then through the second stitch on the knit needle from back to front. Pull the yarn up snugly and drop the first knit stitch off the end of the needle. Bring the yarn to the back and pass through the first stitch on the purl needle from back to front, then through the second stitch on the purl needle from front to back. Pull the yarn up snugly and drop the first purl stitch off the end of the needle. Repeat from * until all stitches have been worked.

As you work, you'll have to continue to move stitches onto the "knit" and "purl" needles—when you have 1 knit and 1 purl stitch remaining, separate and move the knits and purls from the next needle.

Heel Choices

There are several different types of heels that can be used in sock knitting. Some work best for toe-up socks, while others work best for cuff-down socks. There are some heels that can work with either method. Review your heel options here.

Common, or Square, Heel

This is the standard heel that is used on most socks. A heel flap is usually worked in rows on half of the leg stitches for a plain heel, plus or minus a stitch for a balanced pattern. This heel is worked with a slipped stitch at each edge for picking up to form the gusset. For some patterns a slipped stitch is worked at the beginning of each row, and for others the slipped stitch is worked at the beginning and end of every other row. Once the heel flap is knit, it is turned by working short rows across all the stitches on the heel. Stitches are picked up along both sides of the flap and across the instep stitches; gussets are formed with decreases.

Short-Row Heel

This heel is usually worked on half of the stitches while the other half are held for the instep. The first half of the heel is worked by knitting across the heel, then working fewer stitches on each subsequent row. The second half is worked by knitting the center heel stitches, then working more stitches on subsequent rows until you once again work across the entire heel.

Afterthought Heel

Instead of turning the heel while knitting the sock, you can knit a piece of scrap yarn into the sock, marking the heel stitches, then continue up to the cuff in toe-up construction or down to the toe in cuff-down construction. Upon completion of the sock, the waste yarn is removed one stitch at a time and the leg and the foot stitches are placed on needles. The heel is then formed with short row shaping or decreases. When complete, the remaining stitches are grafted together with Kitchener stitch (see pages 38–40). The *Thrummed House Socks* on page 102 are worked from the cuff down and the *Textured Stripe Socks* on page 82 are worked from the toe up, but the heel is worked in the same manner on both pairs of socks.

Gusset

Although not a heel itself, but part of a heel, the gusset is the triangular section that connects the heel stitches of a common heel to the instep stitches. The chain stitches along the sides of the common heel are picked up and joined to the instep and heel stitches. The picked-up stitches are usually decreased on the last two stitches prior to or after working the instep. They are reduced until the total number of heel and gusset stitches equals the number of instep stitches.

Toe Choices

◇◇◇◇◇◇◇◇◇◇◇◇◇◇◇◇◇◇◇◇◇◇◇◇◇◇◇◇◇◇◇◇◇

Just as there are several different types of heels, there are
also several different types of toes that can be used in
sock knitting. Also like heels, different toes can be used
for different sock-knitting methods. Review your toe
options here.

Six-Point Spiral

This shaping is worked on a sock that has a multiple of
six stitches. The decreases form a spiral pattern around
the end of the foot and continue until only six stitches
remain. Finish this toe by Drawing Up the remaining
stitches (see page 37).

Pinwheel Toe

This shaping is used for a toe-up sock. Following a
Circular Cast On (see page 30), stitches are increased
at the beginning of each of the needles, forming four
points as in a pinwheel, until the total number of foot
stitches is reached.

Staggered Spiral Toe

This toe is worked on a multiple of seven stitches plus one. Each round begins with a single knit stitch—this first stitch forms the spiral. For the first decrease round, the decreases are worked at the end of each set of seven stitches; for the second decrease round, the decreases are worked at the end of each set of six stitches; for each following round, the sets of stitches is decreased by one. Continue decreasing until eight stitches remain. This toe is finished by Drawing Up the remaining stitches (see page 37).

Flat Toe

This is the most common way to shape a toe. With an equal number of instep and sole stitches, decrease at both sides of the foot. Kitchener stitch is used to join the remaining stitches (see pages 38–40).

Caring for Hand-Knit Socks

Taking proper care of hand-knit items will ensure them a long and happy life. Follow these easy steps with all of your socks and you'll get to wear them for years to come.

Washing and Blocking

Follow the manufacturer's instructions found on the yarn band for cleaning the yarn or yarns used in your socks. Some yarns are machine washable; others should be washed by hand. Machine washable yarns are best cleaned on a gentle cycle with warm water and a mild soap. Hand wash delicate fibers in a sink or a basin, soaking them in warm water with a mild soap. Squeeze the suds through the socks, then rinse until all the soap is removed. Gently squeeze out as much water as you can (do not wring!) and place the socks in a washing machine on the spin cycle for a few minutes. Remove from the machine and place on sock blockers or a towel to dry. After a few hours, flip socks over onto dry fabric. Socks will usually dry in a day's time.

Storage

Always clean your socks prior to storing them. Here's an old trick I learned years ago for woolen storage: Line a container with fresh newsprint, then cover the newsprint with plain tissue paper. Insert the woolen item (in this case socks) and cover with plain tissue paper. Finally, add another layer of fresh newsprint. The story here is that there is something in the ink on the newsprint that repels moths. Maybe it's an old wives' tale—I only know that it works. Change the newsprint seasonally.

Repair

There is no better explanation of repairing socks than that written by Mary Thomas in her book, *Mary Thomas's Knitting Book,* originally published in 1938. See this book for information on sock repair. More information on this book and others can be found in the *Bibliography* on page 109.

Chapter Three

Projects

Ready to put all of this sock knowledge to use? On the following pages you'll find detailed instructions for thirteen very different pairs of socks. The designs are for plain socks and fancy socks, and there are styles for both women and men. The patterns give details on the exact yarn used for the socks shown, but you should feel free to choose from the many yarns available—just be sure you like the feel of the yarn when it's knitted at the specified gauge. Each pattern includes a secret about the techniques used, and I hope you can bring these methods into all of your sock-knitting adventures!

FISHNET STOCKINGS

Reminiscent of the fishnets popular in the 1960s, these knee-high open-work socks look great with slacks or a skirt. Shown here in classic black, they would also be fun in bright colors. You'll have to do some fancy needlework to keep the correct stitch count, but that's all spelled out in the instructions.

Finished Size
Approx 8" (20cm) circumference, leg and foot length as desired.

Yarn
3 (1¾oz./50g, 191yd./175m) skeins fingering weight yarn

Note: The project shown at right was made using 3 skeins of Rowan 4 Ply Soft (100% merino wool, 1¾oz./50g, 191yd./175m), color 383.

Needles
Set of 5 US 5 (3.75mm) dpns, or size needed to obtain gauge

Set of 5 US 3 (3.25 mm) dpns, or size needed to obtain gauge

Notions
Tapestry needle

Gauge
24 sts = 4" (10cm) in Fishnet Lace on larger needles, unstretched

28 sts = 4" (10cm) in St st on smaller needles

Fishnet Lace Pattern

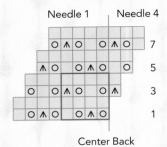

Needle 1 **Needle 4**

7
5
3
1

Center Back

☐ knit

☐ yarn over

Λ slip 2 together knitwise, knit 1, pass 2 slipped stitches over the knit stitch

☐ pattern repeat

Special Stitches

Fishnet Lace Pattern (multiple of 4 sts)

RND 1: *Yo, sl 2 tog kwise, k1, p2sso, yo, k1; rep from * to end of rnd.
RNDS 2 and 4: K all sts.
RND 3: Sl first st from Needle 1 to Needle 4. *Yo, k1, yo, sl 2 tog kwise, k1, p2sso; rep from * to end of rnd.

Note: When you get to the last 2 sts on each needle, you will have to move the first stitch from the next needle to this needle to complete the double decrease.

Rep Rnds 1–4 for patt.

K1, P1 Rib (multiple of 2 sts)

RND 1: *K1, p1; rep from * to end of rnd.
Rep Rnd 1 for patt.

Knit the Leg

Using the Long-Tail Cast On (see page 25) and larger dpns, CO 48 sts and distribute evenly onto 4 dpns. Join into a round taking care not to twist the sts; change to smaller dpns and work K1, P1 Rib for 1" (3cm).
Change to larger dpns and beg Fishnet Lace Pattern. Continue until Leg measures 13" (33cm) or desired length to top of Heel.

Divide for the Heel

With smaller dpns, k 12 sts from Needle 1. Turn and p these 12 plus the 12 sts on Needle 4 onto the same needle. Work these sts back and forth with smaller dpns. Leave rem 24 sts on hold for the Instep.

Knit the Heel Flap

ROW 1 (RS): *Sl 1 pwise, k1; rep from * to end, turn.
ROW 2 (WS): Sl 1 pwise, p to end, turn.
Rep Rows 1–2 eleven more times. You now have 12 chain sts along each side of the Heel Flap.

Turn the Heel

ROW 1 (RS): K17, SSK, turn.
ROW 2 (WS): Sl 1 pwise, p10, p2tog, turn.
ROW 3: Sl 1 kwise, k10, SSK, turn.
Rep Rows 2–3 until all sts have been worked and 12 heel sts rem. End on a WS row, sl the first and last sts of this row (see *This Sock's Secret* on page 77).

Knit the Gussets

Note: Pick up and k through both loops of chain sts.

With the same needle that holds the 12 heel sts, pick up and k 12 chain sts along one side of the Heel Flap.
With larger needle, work the instep sts in Fishnet Lace Pattern as est.
With smaller needle, pick up and k 12 chain sts along the other side of the Heel Flap, then k 6 heel sts onto the same needle.
You now have 18 sts on Needle 1 (smaller dpn), 12 sts each on Needles 2 and 3 (larger needles) and 18 sts on Needle 4 (smaller needle). Continue working gusset and sole sts in St st on smaller needles and instep sts in Fishnet Lace Pattern on larger needles.

Note: For Rnd 3 of Fishnet Lace Pattern, sl the first st onto the previous needle and pass the last st on that needle over this st. Work to last 2 sts, sl 1, k1, psso.

This Sock's Secret

A lace or openwork sock is lovely to knit and wear, but won't hold up well to a lot of wear and tear unless you take special precautions. For added durability and comfort, knit the heel, toe and sole in a sturdier stitch, such as Stockinette stitch on a smaller needle.

Shape the Gussets
RND 1: K to last 2 sts on Needle 1, k2tog; work instep sts in patt as est; SSK at beg of Needle 4, k to end of rnd.
RND 2: K gusset sts and work instep sts in est patt.
Rep Rnds 1–2 until 48 sts rem—12 sts on each needle.

Knit the Foot
Continue working Sole in St st on smaller needles and Instep in Fishnet Lace Pattern on larger needles until foot measures 7½" (19cm) from back of Heel or 2" (5cm) less than desired finished measurement.

Shape the Toe
K all sts onto smaller dpns, discontinuing Fishnet Lace Pattern and working all sts in St st.
RND 1: K to last 3 sts on Needle 1, k2tog, k1; k1, SSK at beg of Needle 2, k to end; k to last 3 sts on Needle 3, k2tog, k1; k1, SSK at beg of Needle 4, k to end.
RND 2: K all sts.
Rep Rnds 1–2 until 4 sts rem on each needle.
K 4 sts from Needle 1 onto Needle 4. Sl 4 sts from Needle 3 onto Needle 2.

Finishing
Kitchener stitch the two sets of 8 sts together (see pages 38–40).
Weave in ends. Wash and block the completed socks. Wear in good health!

LACE CUFF AND CABLE SOCKS

A delicate, ruffled cuff and lovely lace pattern make this sock pretty and playful. The only thing that could make this sock more feminine would be to knit it in pink.

Finished Size
Approx 8" (20cm) circumference, leg and foot length as desired.

Yarn
2 (1¾oz./50g, 175yd./160m) skeins fingering weight yarn

Note: The project shown at right was made using 2 skeins of Nordic Fiber Arts Gammelserie (100% wool, 1¾oz./50g, 175yd./160m), color 438.

Needles
Set of 5 US 1½ (2.5mm) dpns, or size needed to obtain gauge

Set of 5 US 3 (3.25mm) dpns, or size needed to obtain gauge

1 US 6 (4mm) straight needle

Notions
Cable needle

Stitch markers

Tapestry needle

Gauge
32 sts = 4" (10cm) in St st on smaller needles

29 sts = 4" (10cm) in St st on larger needles

Special Stitches

Lace Pattern (multiple of 6 sts)

Note: The st count increases and decreases throughout the 4-rnd patt. Only count your sts after Rnd 4.

RND 1: *[K1, yo] four times, k1, p1; rep from * to end of rnd.
RND 2: *K9, p1; rep from * to end of rnd.
RND 3: *SSK, k5, k2tog, p1; rep from * to end of rnd.
RND 4: *K2tog, k3, SSK, p1; rep from * to end of rnd.
Rep Rnds 1–4 for patt.

Cable Pattern (worked over 17 sts)

RNDS 1, 3 and 4: P1, k6, p2, k6, p2.
RND 2: P1, C6R, p2, C6L, p2.
Rep Rnds 1–4 for patt.

P1, K1 Rib (multiple of 2 sts)

RND 1: *P1, k1; rep from * to end of rnd.
Rep Rnd 1 for patt.

Abbreviations

C6R: Place 3 sts onto cn and hold to the back of the work; k the next 3 sts from the left-hand needle; k the 3 sts on the cn.

C6L: Place 3 sts onto cn and hold to the front of the work; k the next 3 sts from the left-hand needle; k the 3 sts on the cn.

Knit the Cuff

Note: To prevent the cast-on edge from being too tight and rolling upwards, it is important to cast on over two needles or a larger size needle.

Using the Two-Needle Long-Tail Cast On (see page 27) and a straight needle, CO 60 sts. Divide the sts onto 4 dpns so there are 12 sts on Needles 1 and 3 and 18 sts on Needles 2 and 4. Join into a round taking care not to twist the sts; pm for beg of rnd.

Note: Round begins at side of leg, not center back.

Work Lace Pattern for 2¼" (6cm) ending on Rnd 4. On the next rnd, dec 6 sts as foll: *P8, p2tog; rep from * to end—54 sts. At the end of this rnd, turn the work in your hand and reverse the knitting direction. This action will allow the cuff to fold down over the ribbing.

Knit the Leg

Change to smaller needles and adjust sts so you have 14 sts on Needles 1, 2 and 3 and 12 sts on Needle 4. Sl the marker and the first st. (This will reduce the small gap that occurs when the work is reversed.) Work P1, K1 Rib for 2" (5cm).
SET-UP RND: Sl marker, [k5, p1] 5 times, pm, p1, k6, p1, p2tog, k6, p2, pm, k5, p1—53 sts.
Adjust sts so you have 12 sts on Needles 1 and 2, 15 sts on Needle 3 and 14 sts on Needle 4.
NEXT RND: Work Rnd 1 of Lace Pattern over 30 sts, sl marker, work Rnd 1 of Cable Pattern over 17 sts, sl marker, work Rnd 1 of Lace Pattern over last 6 sts. Continue working both patt for 4½" (11cm) or desired length from bottom of ribbing, ending on patt Rnd 4.

Divide for the Heel

ROW 1 (RS): K the sts on Needles 1 and 2 onto one needle, turn—24 sts.
ROW 2 (WS): Sl 1 pwise, p23, p 1 st from Needle 4 onto heel needle—25 sts.
Work the Heel Flap back and forth on these 25 sts. Leave rem 28 sts on hold for the Instep.

Knit the Heel Flap

ROW 1 (RS): Sl 1 kwise, k 24.
ROW 2 (WS): Sl 1 pwise, p 24.
Rep Rows 1–2 eleven more times. You now have 12 chain sts along each side of the Heel Flap.

Turn the Heel

ROW 1 (RS): Sl 1 kwise, k12, SKP, k1, turn.
ROW 2 (WS): Sl 1 pwise, p2, p2tog, p1, turn.
ROW 3: Sl 1 kwise, k3, SKP, k1, turn.
ROW 4: Sl 1 pwise, p4, p2tog, p1, turn.
Continue in this manner, working 1 more st before the dec on every row, until all heel sts have been worked and 13 heel sts rem. K 1 RS row, sl the first and last sts (see *This Sock's Secret* on page 77).

Knit the Gussets

Note: Pick up and k through both loops of chain sts.

With the same needle that holds the 13 heel sts, pick up and k 12 chain sts along one side of the Heel Flap and 1 st in the corner before instep sts. Work in est patt across instep sts. With a new needle, pick up and k 1 st in corner after instep sts and 12 chain sts along other side of the Heel Flap, then k 7 heel sts onto same needle.

Note: Round now begins in the center of the heel. You have 19 sts on Needle 1, 15 sts on Needle 2, 13 sts on Needle 3 and 20 sts on Needle 4—67 sts.

Shape the Gussets

RND 1: K to last 2 sts on Needle 1, p2tog; on Needle 2 work Lace Pattern on first 6 sts, p1, C6R, p2; on Needle 3 C6L, p2, work Lace Pattern over 5 sts, eliminating the ending p1; on Needle 4 p2tog, k to end.

RND 2: K to last st on Needle 1, p1; work Lace and Cable Patterns over Needles 2 and 3 as est; on Needle 4, p1, k to end.

Rep Rnds 1–2 until 14 sts rem on Needle 1 and 15 sts rem on Needle 4.

Knit the Foot

Work even in patt as est until foot measures 7" (18cm) from back of heel or 2½" (6cm) less than desired finished measurement, ending on patt Rnd 4. K 1 rnd, dec 1 st on Needle 4—56 sts.

Shape the Toe

RND 1: K to last 3 sts on Needle 1, k2tog, k1; k1, SSK at beg of Needle 2, k to end; k to last 3 sts on Needle 3, k2tog, k1; k1, SSK at beg of Needle 4, k to end.

RND 2: K all sts.

Rep Rnds 1–2 until 3 sts rem on each needle.

K 3 sts from Needle 1 onto Needle 4. Sl 3 sts from Needle 3 onto Needle 2.

Finishing

Kitchener stitch the two sets of 6 sts together (see pages 38–40).

Weave in ends. Wash and block the completed socks. Wear in good health!

This Sock's Secret

Hiding some ribbing under the lace cuff keeps this sock perfectly pretty, but still perfectly fitted. The ribbing will help hold the sock up on your leg.

PLAITED CABLE SOCKS

These classic cabled socks are sure to become a staple in your wardrobe. Because they are worked in worsted weight yarn, they are quick to knit and also thick, warm and cozy. Try them in a classic color, like the gray pair shown here, or strike out in a new direction with a bold color choice.

Finished Size
Approx 9" (23cm) circumference, leg and foot length as desired.

Yarn
2 (3½oz./100g, 220yd./200m) skeins worsted weight yarn

Note: The project shown at right was made using 2 skeins of Cascade Yarn Cascade 220 (100% wool, 3½oz./100g, 220yd./200m), color 8400.

Needles
Set of 5 US 4 (3.5mm) dpns, or one size smaller than larger needles

Set of 5 US 5 (3.75mm) dpns, or size needed to obtain gauge

1 US 5 (3.75mm) straight needle

Notions
Cable needle

Stitch markers

Tapestry needle

Gauge
24 sts = 4" (10cm) in St st on larger needles

Special Stitches

9-Stitch Cable (worked over 64 sts)

RNDS 1 and 5: [P2, k9, p2, k1, p1, k1] four times.
RNDS 2, 4, 6 and 8: [P2, k9, p2, k3] four times.
RND 3: [P2, C6L, k3, p2, k1, p1, k1, p2, k3, C6R, p2, k1, p1, k1] two times.
RND 7: [P2, k3, C6R, p2, k1, p1, k1, p2, C6L, k3, p2, k1, p1, k1] two times.
Rep Rnds 1–8 for patt.

6-Stitch Cable (worked over 29 sts)

RNDS 1 and 5: K1, p1, k1, [p2, k6, p2, k1, p1, k1] two times.
RNDS 2, 4, 6 and 8: K1, p1, k1, [p2, k6, p2, k3] two times.
RND 3: K1, p1, k1, p2, C4L, k2, p2, k1, p1, k1, p2, k2, C4R, p2, k1, p1, k1.
RND 7: K1, p1, k1, p2, k2, C4R, p2, k1, p1, k1, p2, C4L, k2, p2, k1, p1, k1.
Rep Rnds 1–8 for patt.

K2, P2 Rib (multiple of 4 sts)

RND 1: *K2, p2; rep from * to end of rnd.
Rep Rnd 1 for patt.

Abbreviations

C6R: Place 3 sts onto cn and hold to the back of the work; k the next 3 sts from the left-hand needle; k the 3 sts on the cn.

C6L: Place 3 sts onto cn and hold to the front of the work; k the next 3 sts from the left-hand needle; k the 3 sts on the cn.

C4R: Place 2 sts onto cn and hold to the back of the work; k the next 2 sts from the left-hand needle; k the 2 sts on the cn.

C4L: Place 2 sts onto cn and hold to the front of the work; k the next 2 sts from the left-hand needle; k the 2 sts on the cn.

Knit the Leg

Using the Patterned Cast On (see page 27) and a straight needle, CO 64 sts in K2, P2 Rib. Distribute evenly onto 4 smaller dpns (16 sts per needle) and join into a round taking care not to twist the sts. Work K2, P2 Rib for 2½" (6cm).

Note: Round begins at side of leg, not center back.

Change to larger dpns. Work 9-Stitch Cable for about 8" (20cm) or desired length to top of Heel, ending on Rnd 8.

Divide for the Heel

Sl 13 sts from Needle 2 onto Needle 1—29 sts. Leave rem 35 sts on hold for the Instep.

Knit the Heel Flap

ROW 1 (RS): Sl 1 pwise, [p2, k1, p1, k1] five times, p2, k1.
ROW 2 (WS): Sl 1 pwise, [k2, p3] five times, k2, p1.
Rep Rows 1–2 ten more times. You now have 11 chain sts along each side of the Heel Flap.

Turn the Heel

ROW 1 (RS): Sl 1 kwise, k15, SSK, k1, turn.
ROW 2 (WS): Sl 1 pwise, p5, p2tog, p1, turn.
ROW 3: Sl 1 kwise, k6, SSK, k1, turn.
ROW 4: Sl 1 pwise, p7, p2tog, p1, turn.
Continue in this manner, working 1 more st before the dec on every row, until all sts have been worked and 17 heel sts rem. K 1 RS row, sl the first and last sts of this row (see *This Sock's Secret* on page 77).

Knit the Gussets

Note: Instep sts are reduced on the first rnd. This dec rnd is not repeated. Hereafter the 6-Stitch Cable patt is worked as given above.

Note: Pick up and k through both loops of chain sts.

With the same needle that holds the heel sts, pick up and k 11 chain sts along one side of the Heel Flap. With a new needle, work as foll across instep sts: K1, p1, k1, *p2, [k1, k2tog] three times, p2, k1, p1, k1; rep from * two times—29 sts rem on the Instep. With a new needle, pick up and k 11 chain sts along the other side of the Heel Flap, then k 8 heel sts onto the same needle. You now have 20 sts on Needle 1, 29 sts on Needle 2, and 19 sts on Needle 3—68 sts. You are now working on three needles.

Shape the Gussets

RND 1: K to last 2 sts on Needle 1, SSK; work instep sts in 6-Stitch Cable, beg with Rnd 2 of patt; on Needle 3, k2tog, k to end.

RND 2: K all sts on Needle 1; work instep sts in patt as est on Needle 2; on Needle 3, k to end.

Rep Rnds 1–2 until 16 sts rem on Needle 1 and 15 sts rem on Needle 3.

Knit the Foot

Continue working sole sts in St st and instep sts in 6-Stitch Cable until foot measures 7½" (19cm) from back of heel or 2" (5cm) less than desired finished measurement, ending on Rnd 1 or 5 of patt.

Shape the Toe

Discontinue 6-Stitch Cable and work all sts in St st. Redistribute sts equally onto 4 needles.

RND 1: K to last 3 sts on Needle 1, k2tog, k1; k1, SSK at beg of Needle 2, k to end; k to last 3 sts on Needle 3, k2tog, k1; k1, SSK at beg of Needle 4, k to end.

RND 2: K all sts.

Rep Rnds 1–2 until 4 sts rem on each needle.

K 4 sts from Needle 1 onto Needle 4. Sl 4 sts from Needle 3 onto Needle 2.

Finishing

Kitchener stitch the two sets of 8 sts together (see pages 38–40).

Weave in ends. Wash and block the completed socks. Wear in good health!

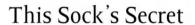

This Sock's Secret

A cable can be a bulky feature in a sock, and large cables can be uncomfortable on the foot of a sock inside a shoe. The nine-stitch plaited cable on the leg of this sock changes to a six-stitch plaited cable to reduce the bulk on top of the foot.

SEA SQUALL SOCKS
with Mango Madness Variation

The unusual construction of this sock sets it apart from others. Try this sock when you're in the mood for a unique knitting experience. For a similar sock with traditional construction, try the Mango Madness Variation on page 66.

Finished Size
Approx 9" (23cm) circumference, approx 5½" (14cm) leg length, foot length as desired.

Yarn
1 (4oz./113g, 560yd./512m) skein fingering weight yarn

Note: The project shown at right was made using 1 skein of Schaefer Yarn Company Anne (60% superwash merino wool/25% mohair/15% nylon, 4oz./113g, 560yd./512m), in the Sea Tones colorway.

Needles
Set of 5 US 1½ (2.5mm) dpns, or size needed to obtain gauge

US 3 (3.25mm) straight needles

US D (3.25mm) crochet hook

Notions
Cotton waste yarn

Tapestry needle

Gauge
36 sts = 4" (10cm) in St st on dpns

Special Stitches

Wave Pattern (multiple of 6 sts + 5)

Note: Sl all sts pwise. Odd rows are WS rows, even rows are RS rows.

ROWS 1, 3 and 8: Sl 1, *k3, p3; rep from * to last 4 sts, k4.
ROWS 2, 7 and 9: Sl 1, *p3, k3; rep from * to last 4 sts, p4.
ROWS 4, 6 and 11: Sl 1, p to end.
ROWS 5, 10 and 12: Sl 1, k to end.
Rep Rows 1–12 for patt.

Knit the Leg

Using the Provisional Crochet Cast On (see page 28), straight needles and waste yarn, CO 53 sts. With main yarn, k 1 row. Work flat in Wave Pattern until piece measures approx 9" (23cm) or fits comfortably around the ankle, ending with Row 10 of patt.
Undo crochet chain, placing live sts on straight needle. Graft live sts together using Kitchener stitch (see pages 38–40).

Note: Pick up and k through both loops of chain sts.

Using dpns, pick up and k 66 sts around the edge of the Leg—17 sts on Needles 1 and 3, and 16 sts on Needles 2 and 4. K 1 rnd.

Divide for the Heel

K sts from Needle 1 onto Needle 4 to beg Heel Flap—33 sts. Leave rem 33 sts on hold for the Instep.

Turn the Heel

ROW 1 (WS): K all sts.
ROW 2 (RS): *Sl 1 pwise, k1; rep from * to last st, bring yarn to front, sl the last st.
Rep Rows 1–2 sixteen more times, ending on a RS row. You now have 17 chain sts along each side of the Heel Flap.

Turn the Heel

ROW 1 (WS): P18, p2tog, p1, turn.
ROW 2 (RS): Sl 1 kwise, k4, SSK, k1, turn.
ROW 3: Sl 1 pwise, p5, p2tog, p1, turn.
ROW 4: Sl 1 kwise, k6, SSK, k1, turn.

Continue in this manner, working 1 more st before the dec on every row, until all sts have been worked and 19 heel sts rem. End on a WS row.

Knit the Gussets

With the same needle that holds the heel sts, pick up and k 17 chain sts along one side of the Heel Flap. K across instep sts on Needles 2 and 3. With a new needle, pick up and k 17 chain sts along the other side of the Heel Flap, then k 9 heel sts onto the same needle—86 sts.

Shape the Gussets

RND 1: K to last 3 sts on Needle 1, k2tog, k1; k instep sts on Needles 2 and 3; k1, SSK at beg of Needle 4, k to end.
RND 2: K all sts.
Rep Rnds 1–2 until 17 sts rem on Needle 1 and 16 sts rem on Needle 4—66 sts.

Knit the Foot

Continue working in St st until foot measures about 7½" (19cm) from back of the Heel or 1½" (4cm) less than desired finished measurement.

Shape the Toe

RND 1: *K9, k2tog; rep from * to end of rnd—60 sts.
EVEN RNDS 2–12: K all sts.
RND 3: *K8, k2tog; rep from * to end of rnd—54 sts.
RND 5: *K7, k2tog; rep from * to end of rnd—48 sts.
RND 7: *K6, k2tog; rep from * to end of rnd—42 sts.
RND 9: *K5, k2tog; rep from * to end of rnd—36 sts.
RND 11: *K4, k2tog; rep from * to end of rnd—30 sts.
RND 13: *K3, k2tog; rep from * to end of rnd—24 sts.
RND 14: *K2, k2tog; rep from * to end of rnd—18 sts.
RND 15: *K1, k2tog; rep from * to end of rnd—12 sts.
RND 16: *K2tog; rep from * to end of rnd—6 sts.

Finishing

Break yarn, leaving a 10" (25cm) tail. Thread the tail onto the tapestry needle and draw it through the rem sts. Pull up snug and fasten off.
Weave in ends. Wash and block the completed socks. Wear in good health!

This Sock's Secret

Working the leg vertically takes this sock in a whole new direction. Try this construction method with any pattern. Cast on, work in pattern, then graft the stitches together to form a tube. Pick up stitches along the bottom of the tube to form the foot, and you'll have a unique and imaginative pair of socks.

MANGO MADNESS
Variation

Finished Size
Approx 8" (20cm) circumference, leg and foot length as desired.

Yarn
1 (4oz./113g, 560yd./512m) skein fingering weight yarn

The project shown at right was made using 1 skein of Schaefer Yarn Company Anne (60% superwash merino wool/25% mohair/15% nylon, 4oz./113g, 560yd./512m), in the Mango Tones colorway.

Needles
Set of 5 US 1 (2.25mm) dpns, or one size smaller than larger needles

Set of 5 US 1½ (2.5mm) dpns, or size needed to obtain gauge

1 US 1 (2.25mm) straight needle

16" (40cm) US 1 (2.25mm) circular needle

Notions
Cotton waste yarn

Stitch markers

Tapestry needle

Gauge
36 sts = 4" (10cm) in St st on larger needles

Special Stitches

Leg Pattern (multiple of 6 sts)

RNDS 1–3: P all sts.
RNDS 4–6: *K3, p3; rep from * to end of rnd.
RNDS 7–9: K all sts.
RNDS 10–12: *P3, k3; rep from * to end of rnd.
Rep Rnds 1–12 for patt.

Foot Pattern (worked over 37 sts)

RNDS 1–3: P5, [k3, p3] four times, k3, p5.
RNDS 4–6: P2, [k3, p3] five times, k3, p2.
Rep Rnds 1–6 for patt.

Knit the Leg
Using the Invisible Provisional Cast On (see page 29), a straight needle, and main yarn with waste yarn, CO 72 sts. Using main yarn, work 1 row in K1, P1 rib, dropping slip knot at end of row. Divide the sts evenly onto 4 smaller dpns. Join into a rnd taking care not to twist the sts; pm for beg of rnd.

Inside Cuff Ribbing
RNDS 1–14: *K1, p1; rep from * to end of rnd. Change to larger dpns. Work Rnds 1–12 of Leg Pattern, then work Rnds 1–8 of Leg Pattern—20 patt rnds total.

Joining Round
Place provisional CO sts onto circular needle, remove waste yarn, and fold the rib rnds to the inside of Leg Pattern rnds.
To join the K1, P1 rib facing to the inside of the leg, k 1 leg st on dpns tog with 1 provisional CO st from circular needle.
Continue in patt until leg measures 5½" (14cm) unstretched, or desired leg length to top of Heel, ending on Rnd 8.

Divide for the Heel
K 18 sts on Needle 1. K 18 sts on Needle 2 and 18 sts on Needle 3 plus 1 st from Needle 4—37 sts for the Instep. Place 35 sts from Needles 1 and 4 on a single needle for the Heel Flap.

Knit the Heel Flap
ROW 1 (RS): *Sl 1 pwise, k1; rep from * to last st, bring yarn to front of work, sl last st pwise.
ROW 2 (WS): K all sts.
Rep Rows 1–2 seventeen more times, ending on a RS row. You now have 18 chain sts along each side of the Heel Flap.

Turn the Heel

ROW 1 (WS): P19, p2tog, p1, turn.
ROW 2 (RS): Sl 1 kwise, k4, SSK, k1, turn.
ROW 3: Sl 1 pwise, p5, p2tog, p1, turn.
ROW 4: Sl 1 kwise, k6, SSK, k1, turn.
Continue in this manner, working 1 more st before the dec on every row, until all heel sts have been worked and 19 heel sts rem. End on a WS row, sl the first and last st of this row (see *This Sock's Secret* on page 77).

Knit the Gussets

Note: Pick up and k through both loops of chain sts.

With the same needle that holds the heel sts, pick up and k 18 chain sts along one side of the Heel Flap. Work instep sts on Needles 2 and 3 in Foot Pattern. With a new needle, pick up and k 18 chain sts along other side of the Heel Flap, then k 9 heel sts onto the same needle—92 sts.

Shape the Gussets

RND 1: K to last 3 sts on Needle 1, k2tog, k1. Work instep sts in Foot Pattern as est; k1, SSK at the beg of Needle 4, k to end.
RND 2: K gusset sts and work instep sts in patt as est.
Rep Rnds 1–2 until 18 sts rem on Needle 1 and 17 sts rem on Needle 4—72 sts total.

Knit the Foot

Continue working sole sts in St st and Instep in Foot Pattern until the foot measures 7" (18cm) from back of Heel or 2" (5cm) less than desired finished length.

Shape the Toe

K 1 rnd, moving last st on Needle 3 to Needle 4.
RND 1: K to last 3 sts on Needle 1, k2tog, k1; k1, SSK at beg of Needle 2, k to end; k to last 3 sts on Needle 3, k2tog, k1; k1, SSK at beg of Needle 4, k to end.
RND 2: K all sts.
Rep Rnds 1–2 until 9 sts rem on each needle.
Rep Rnd 1 only four times—5 sts rem on each needle.
K 5 sts from Needle 1 onto Needle 4. Sl 5 sts from Needle 3 onto Needle 2.

Finishing

Kitchener stitch the two sets of 10 sts together (see pages 38-40).
Weave in ends. Wash and block the completed socks. Wear in good health!

This Sock's Secret

This scrunchy sock begins with an invisible provisional crochet cast on that extends into a snug K1, P1 inner rib. You don't have to worry about your socks falling down—the inner K1, P1 ribbing keeps them snug.

RIBBED BOOT SOCKS

This is a classic boot sock that you'll want to knit in every color! Use a durable yarn in a great colorway and your socks will not only look great, they'll also last as long as your boots.

Finished Size

Approx 9" (23cm) circumference, leg and foot length as desired.

Yarn

2 (3½oz./100g, 350yd./320m) skeins DK weight yarn

Note: The project shown at right was made using 2 skeins of Mountain Colors Bearfoot (60% superwash wool/25% mohair/15% nylon, 3½oz./100g, 350yd./320m), color Wilderness.

Needles

Set of 5 US 2½ (3mm) dpns, or one size smaller than larger needles

Set of 5 US 3 (3.25 mm) dpns, or size needed to obtain gauge

1 US 3 (3.25mm) straight needle

1 extra US 2½ (3mm) dpn for cast on

Notions

Cotton waste yarn

Ravel cord

Stitch markers

Tapestry needle

Gauge

28 sts = 4" (10cm) in St st on larger needles

Special Stitches

K2, P2 Rib

RND 1: *K2, p2; rep from * to end of rnd.
Rep Rnd 1 for patt.

Knit the Leg

Using the Rolled Edge Cast On (see page 26), CO 32 sts working main yarn on smaller needle.

Note: Round begins at side of leg, not center back.

This CO produces a K1, P1 edge. To change to K2, P2 Rib, proceed as foll: *With 2 empty dpns held parallel, sl the sts off Needle 1, placing all the k sts on the front empty needle and all the p sts on the back empty needle. **K 2 sts from the needle with the k sts and p 2 sts from the needle with the p sts; rep from ** to end of needle. Rep from * over sts on rem needles. Work K2, P2 Rib for 3" (8cm).
Change to larger needles and continue in ribbing for 9" (23cm) more. The leg should measure approx 12" (30cm).

Divide for the Heel

Place 32 sts from Needles 3 and 4 on holder for the Instep. Place rem 32 sts on 1 dpn and work short-row heel as foll:

First Half of Heel

ROW 1 (RS): K31, wrap st, turn.
ROW 2 (WS): P30, wrap st, turn.
ROW 3: K29, wrap st, turn.
ROW 4: P28, wrap st, turn.
Continue in this manner, working 1 less st before each wrap st on every row until you have 9 wrapped sts on each side and 14 unwrapped sts in the center, ending on a WS row.

Second Half of Heel

ROW 1 (RS): K the 14 unwrapped sts. When you reach the first wrapped st, k the wrap tog with the st. Wrap the next st. (This st will now have 2 wraps.) Turn.
ROW 2 (WS): P to next wrapped st—15 sts. P wrap tog with st. Wrap the next st. (This st will now have 2 wraps.) Turn.
ROW 3: K to double wrapped st. K both wraps together with st. Wrap next st. Turn.
ROW 4: P to double wrapped st. P both wraps together with st. Wrap next st. Turn.
Continue working outward in this manner until all the sts have been worked, ending on a RS row.

Knit the Foot

Change to smaller needles, placing 32 heel sts on two needles. Beg working St st and continue until the foot measures 9" (23cm), or 2" (5cm) less than desired finished measurement.

Shape the Toe

RND 1: K1, SSK at beg of Needle 1, k to end; k to last 3 sts on Needle 2, k2tog, k1; k1, SSK at beg of Needle 3, k to end; k to last 3 sts on Needle 4, k2tog, k1.
RND 2: K all sts.
Rep Rnds 1–2 until 8 sts rem on each needle, then work Rnd 1 only four more times until 4 sts rem on each needle. Sl 4 sts from Needle 2 onto Needle 1. Sl 4 sts from Needle 3 onto Needle 4.

Finishing

Kitchener stitch the two sets of 8 sts together (see pages 38–40).
Weave in ends. Wash and block the completed socks. Wear in good health!

This Sock's Secret

A short-row heel like the one used in this pattern is a great addition to any sock, toe up or cuff down. See page 42 for more information about short row heels. If the heel becomes worn, it is easy to replace.

TRAVELING STITCH SOCKS

Wear this pair with your kilt or for clogging! These lovely traditional-looking socks use a traveling stitch pattern. Traveling stitch patterns are usually worked without a cable needle, but I found it much easier to work with a cable needle on these small stitches.

Finished Size

Approx 8" (20cm) circumference, leg and foot length as desired.

Yarn

2 (4oz./113g, 420yd./384m) skeins fingering weight yarn

Note: The project shown at right was made using 2 skeins of Cherry Tree Hill Yarn Supersock Solids (100% merino wool, 4oz./113g, 420yd./384m), color Natural.

Needles

Set of 5 US 1½ (2.5mm) dpns, or three sizes smaller than larger needles

Set of 5 US 3 (3.25 mm) dpns, or size needed to obtain gauge

1 US 3 (3.25mm) straight needle

Notions

Cable needle

Stitch markers

Tapestry needle

Gauge

38 sts = 4" (10cm) in St st on larger needles

Traveling Stitch Pattern

Chart A

Repeat

1, 3, 5, 7, 9, 11, 13, 15, 17, 19

Chart B

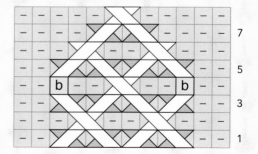

1, 3, 5, 7

Legend

- ☐ knit
- – purl
- b knit in back of stitch
- ＼ slip, slip, knit two stitches together through back loop
- ○ yarn over
- ／ knit two stitches together
- C2L place next stitch on cn and hold in front, k1, k1b from cn
- C2R place next stitch on cn and hold in back, k1b, k1 from cn
- PRC place next stitch on cn and hold in back, k1b, p1 from cn
- PLC place next stitch on cn and hold in front, p1, k1b, from cn

Special Stitches

Twisted Rib

RND 1: *K1 tbl, p1; rep from * to end of rnd.
RND 2: *K1, p1 tbl; rep from * to end of rnd.
Rep Rnds 1–2 for patt.

Traveling Stitch Pattern

Chart A (worked over 25 sts)
RND 1: P1, k1 tbl, p2, SSK, yo, k1, p3, k2 tbl, p2, k2 tbl, p3, k1, yo, k2tog, p2, k1 tbl.
RNDS 2, 6 and 10: K1, k1 tbl, p2, k1, yo, k2tog, p3, C2L, p2, C2L, p3, SSK, yo, k1, p2, k1 tbl.
RNDS 3, 7 and 11: P1, k1 tbl, p2, SSK, yo, k1, p2, [PRC, PLC] twice, p2, k1, yo, k2tog, p2, k1 tbl.
RNDS 4 and 8: K1, k1 tbl, p2, k1, yo, k2tog, p2, k1 tbl, p2, C2L, p2, k1 tbl, p2, SSK, yo, k1, p2, k1 tbl.
RND 5 and 9: P1, k1 tbl, p2, SSK, yo, k1, p2, [PLC, PRC] twice, p2, k1, yo, k2tog, p2, k1 tbl.
RND 12: K1, k1 tbl, p2, k1, yo, k2tog, p2, k1 tbl, p2, C2L, p2, k1 tbl, p2, SSK, yo, k1, p2, k1 tbl.
RND 13: P1, k1 tbl, p2, SSK, yo, k1, p2, k1 tbl, p2, k2 tbl, p2, k1 tbl, p2, k1, yo, k2tog, p2, k1 tbl.
RND 14: K1, k1 tbl, p2, k1, yo, k2tog, p2, k1 tbl, p2, C2L, p2, k1 tbl, p2, SSK, yo, k1, p2, k1 tbl.
RNDS 15–20: Rep Rnds 13–14 three times.

Chart B (worked over 12 sts)
RNDS 1 and 5: P2, [PLC, PRC] twice, p2.
RND 2: P3, C2L, p2, C2L, p3.
RND 3: P2, [PRC, PLC] twice, p2.
RND 4: P2, k1 tbl, p2, C2L, p2, k1 tbl, p2.
RND 6: P3, C2L, p2, C2R, p3.
RND 7: P4, PLC, PRC, p4.
RND 8: P5, C2L, p5.

Knit the Cuff

Using the Patterned Cast On (see page 27) and a straight needle, CO 76 sts in K1, P1 rib. Distribute sts evenly onto 4 smaller needles and join into a round taking care not to twist the sts. Pm for beg of rnd.

Note: Round begins at center back.

Work Twisted Rib for 1¾" (4cm). Dec 1 st on the last rnd—75 sts.

Abbreviations

C2L: Place next st on cn and hold in front of work, k1, k1b tbl from cn.

C2R: Place next st on cn and hold in back of work, k1 tbl, k st from cn.

k1 tbl: K through back loop of the st.

p1 tbl: P through back loop of the st.

PLC: Place next st on cn and hold in front, p1, k1 tbl from cn.

PRC: Place next st on cn and hold in back, k1 tbl, p1 from cn.

Knit the Leg

Change to larger dpns and divide sts evenly onto 3 needles. Work Rnds 1–20 of Traveling Stitch Pattern, Chart A. Rep Rnds 5–20 (16-rnd rep) three more times, then work Rnds 5–12 once or until leg measures 8½" (22cm) below the ribbing or desired length to top of the Heel. Cut yarn.

Divide for the Heel

Sl 19 sts from Needle 1 to Needle 3. Join yarn.
SET-UP ROW (WS): P37, place all rem sts onto Needle 2, turn. Work the Heel Flap back and forth on these 37 sts. Leave rem 38 sts on hold for the Instep.

Knit the Heel Flap

ROW 1 (RS): *Sl 1 pwise, k1 tbl; rep from * to last st, bring yarn to front of work, sl last st pwise.
ROW 2 (WS): P all sts.
Rep Rows 1–2 fourteen more times. You now have 15 chain sts on each edge of the Heel Flap.

Turn the Heel

ROW 1 (RS): K22, SSK, k1, turn.
ROW 2 (WS): Sl 1 pwise, p8, p2tog, p1, turn.
ROW 3: Sl 1 kwise, k9, SSK, k1, turn.
ROW 4: Sl 1 pwise, p10, p2tog, p1, turn.
Continue in this manner, working 1 more st before the dec on every row, until all heel sts have been worked and 23 sts rem. K 1 RS row, sl the first and last sts of this row (see *This Sock's Secret* on page 77).

Knit the Gussets

Note: Pick up and k through both loops of chain sts.

With the same needle that holds the heel sts, pick up and k 15 chain sts along one side of the Heel Flap and 1 st in the corner before instep sts.

With a new needle, work the 38 instep sts in Traveling Stitch Pattern as est; with a new needle, pick up and k 1 st in the corner after instep sts and 15 chain sts along other side of the Heel Flap, then k 11 heel sts onto same needle—93 sts.

Shape the Gussets

RND 1: K to last 2 sts on Needle 1, k2tog, p1 from Needle 2 onto Needle 1; work instep sts in patt as est on Needle 2 to last st, p last st onto Needle 3; SSK at the beg of Needle 3, k to end.

RND 2: K gusset sts and work instep sts in patt as est, maintaining 1 p st on each side of instep sts.

RND 3: K to last 3 sts on Needle 1, k2tog, p1; work instep sts in patt on Needle 2; p1, SSK at beg of Needle 3, k to end.

Rep Rnds 2–3 until 75 sts rem, 19 sts on Needle 1, 38 sts on Needle 2, and 18 sts on Needle 3. Work 1 rnd even, inc 1 st on Needle 3 —76 sts.

Knit the Foot

Continue working sole sts in St st, maintaining 1 p st on each side of instep sts, and instep sts in Traveling Stitch Pattern until foot measures 7½" (19cm) from back of Heel or 2" (5cm) less than desired finished measurement, ending on patt Rnd 20.

Shape the Toe

RND 1 (Dec Rnd): K to last 3 sts on Needle 1, SSK, p1; at beg of Needle 2, p1, k2tog, k10, work Chart B over next 12 sts, k to last 3 sts on Needle 2, SSK, p1; p1, k2tog at beg of Needle 3, k to end.

RND 2: Work even in est patt.

RND 3 (Dec Rnd): K to last 3 sts on Needle 1, SSK, p1; at beg of Needle 2, p1, k2tog, k9, work Chart B over next 12 sts, k to last 3 sts on Needle 2, SSK, p1; p1, k2tog at beg of Needle 3, k to end.

RND 4: Work even in est patt.

Continue in this manner, working one fewer st before and after Chart B sts on each dec rnd six more times—44 sts. Work dec rnd only five times—24 sts.

With Needle 3, k across 6 sts on Needle 1.

Finishing

Kitchener stitch the two sets of 12 sts together (see pages 38–40).

Weave in ends. Wash and block the completed socks.

Wear in good health!

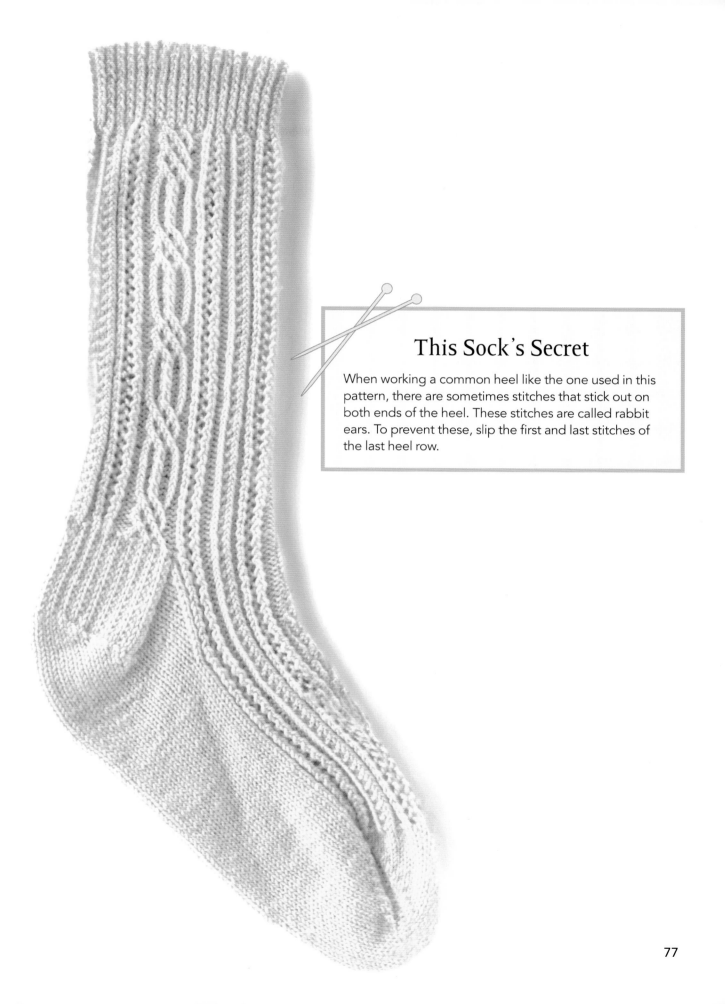

This Sock's Secret

When working a common heel like the one used in this pattern, there are sometimes stitches that stick out on both ends of the heel. These stitches are called rabbit ears. To prevent these, slip the first and last stitches of the last heel row.

BRAID BANDED SOCKS

The tasseled starting points on these socks make them a pair with a right and left. Make sure to work one of each—you don't want to end up with two left feet!

Finished Size
Approx 7½" (19cm) circumference, leg and foot length as desired.

Yarn
3 (1¾oz./50g, 213yd./195m) skeins fingering weight yarn, 1 each of 3 colors (A, B and C)

Note: The project shown at right was made using 3 skeins of SandnesGarn Lanett Superwash, (100% merino wool, 1¾oz./50g, 213yd./195m), 1 each of colors 1012 (A), 5575 (B) and 5846 (C).

Needles
Set of 5 US 2 (2.75mm) dpns, or size needed to obtain gauge

Notions
Tapestry needle
Yarn bobbins

Gauge
32 sts = 4" (10cm) in St st

Special Stitches

Double Seed Stitch (multiple of 7 sts)

RNDS 1 and 2: *[P1, k1] 3 times, p1; rep from * to end of rnd.
RNDS 3 and 4: *[K1, p1] 3 times, k1; rep from * to end of rnd.
Rep Rnds 1–4 for patt.

Knitted-In I-Cord

To set up the I-cords, knit to the place you want an I-cord. With contrasting color, k1, p1, k1 in next stitch. On subsequent rounds, when you get to the I-cord stitches, the yarn will be on the far side of the three stitches. Pick up this yarn, bring it back to the first I-cord stitch and knit the stitches. Bringing the yarn across will cause the I-cord to stand away from the background.

Prepare the Bobbins
Cut five strands of Color C 3½ yd. (3m) long. Cut three strands of Color C 7½ yd. (7m) long. Wind these strands onto bobbins.

Knit the Leg

Both Socks
Holding Colors A and B tog, form a slip stitch and place it on the needle. With Color A over the thumb and Color B over the index finger, CO 64 sts using the Long-Tail Cast On (see page 25). Distribute the sts evenly onto 4 dpns. Drop the slip stitch and join into a round taking care not to twist the sts.

Note: Round begins at side of leg, not center back.

With Color A, k 1 rnd. Work the Two-Color Braided Cast On with Colors A and B (see page 27). Do not cut the yarns. Join Color C and k 1 rnd, p 1 rnd. K 1 rnd Color B. Work the Two-Color Braided Cast On again, but this time work Rnd 2 and then Rnd 1. This will make the Vs of the braids point in opposite directions. Cut Color B, leaving a tail to be woven in later.

Right Sock
With a small bobbin of Color C, k1, p1, k1 in the first st. Work Double Seed Stitch with Color A over next 7 sts. *With a large bobbin of Color C, k1, p1, k1 in the next st. Work Double Seed Stitch with Color A over next 7 sts. Rep from * two more times. **With a small

bobbin of Color C, k1, p1, k1 in the next st. Work Double Seed Stitch with Color A over next 7 sts. Rep from ** three more times—80 sts.

Left Sock
*With a small bobbin of Color C, k1, p1, k1 in the first st. Work Double Seed Stitch with Color A over next 7 sts. Rep from * three more times. With a small bobbin of Color C, k1, p1, k1 in the next st. **Work Double Seed Stitch with Color A over next 7 sts. With a large bobbin of Color C, k1, p1, k1 in the next st. Rep from ** two more times. Work Double Seed Stitch over last 7 sts—80 sts.

Both Socks

Note: When changing colors on subsequent rounds, always bring the new color under the old color.

Continue working Knitted-In I-Cord separated by 7 sts in Double Seed Stitch until Leg measures 5½" (14cm) from beg, or desired length to top of Heel.

Divide for the Heel

Right Sock
Work as est over 37 sts and put on hold for the Instep. Work the next 43 sts as est, k the 3 sts of the five short I-cords together so you have 1 st at the end of these I-cords—33 heel sts. Turn. Join Color B and p 1 WS row.

Left Sock
Work the next 43 sts as est, k the 3 sts of the five short I-cords together so you have 1 st at the end of these I-cords—33 heel sts. Turn. Place rem 37 sts on hold for the Instep. Join Color B and p1 WS row.

Knit the Heel Flap

Note: Both socks are worked the same from here through the end of the patt.

ROW 1 (RS): *Sl 1 pwise, k1; rep from * to last st, k1.
ROW 2 (WS): Sl 1 pwise, p to end.
Rep Rows 1–2 fifteen more times. You now have 16 chain sts on each edge of the Heel Flap.

Turn the Heel
ROW 1 (RS): K19, SSK, k1.
ROW 2 (WS): Sl 1 pwise, p6, p2tog, p1.
ROW 3: Sl 1 pwise, k7, SSK, k1.
ROW 4: Sl 1 pwise, p8, p2tog, p1.
Continue in this manner, working 1 more st before the dec on each row, until 19 sts rem. K 1 RS row, sl the

first and last sts of this row (see *This Sock's Secret* on page 77).
Cut Color B.

Knit the Gussets

Note: Pick up and k through both loops of chain sts.

Join Color A. With the needle that holds the heel sts, pick up and k 16 chain sts along one side of Heel Flap. Work 37 instep sts in est patt. With a new needle, pick up and k 16 chain sts along the other side of the Heel Flap, then k 10 heel sts onto same needle—88 sts.

Note: Round now begins at the center back.

Shape the Gussets
RND 1: K to last 2 sts on Needle 1, k2tog; work instep sts in patt on Needles 2 and 3; SSK at beg of Needle 4, k to end.
RND 2: K gusset sts on Needles 1 and 4 and work instep sts in patt.
Rep Rnds 1–2 until 16 sts rem on Needle 1 and 17 sts rem on Needle 4—70 sts total.

Knit the Foot
Keeping 37 instep sts in patt as est and working 33 sole sts in St st, work even until the foot measures 6"

(15cm) from back of Heel or 2" (5cm) less than desired finished length.

Shape the Toe
RND 1: K to the last 2 sts of Needle 1, k2tog; work Needles 2 and 3 in patt, dec 1 st in each Double Seed Stitch section; SSK at beg of Needle 4, k to end.
RND 2: Work even as est.
Rep Rnds 1–2 until 10 sts rem. On the last rnd, dec ea I-cord to 1st.

Finishing
Break yarn, leaving a 10" (25cm) tail. Thread the tail onto the tapestry needle and draw it through the rem sts. Pull up snug and fasten off.
To create a tassel, cut two 30" (76cm) strands of each color. Hold the strands together, fold them in half and draw the folded ends through the cuff. Pull the cut ends through the looped ends and pull them snug. Braid the strands together for the desired length and secure with an overhand knot. Trim the ends even. Weave in ends. Wash and block the completed socks. Wear in good health!

This Sock's Secret

The I-cords that make the vertical stripes are knitted in as you go. This clever technique makes you look like an expert while the pattern is really quite simple.

TEXTURED STRIPE SOCKS

These handsome socks feature four different textured patterns on the leg. The socks are knit from the toe up, ending with a narrow striped rib at the cuff.

Finished Size

Approx 8" (20cm) circumference, leg and foot length as desired.

Yarn

5 (1¾oz./50g, 142yd./130m) skeins DK weight yarn, 1 each of 5 colors (A, B, C, D and E)

Note: The project shown at right was made using 5 skeins of Rowan Cashsoft DK (57% extra fine merino wool/33% microfiber/10% cashmere, 1¾oz./50g, 142yd./130m), 1 each of colors 517 (A), 522 (B), 513 (C), 515 (D) and 500 (E).

Needles

Set of 5 US 2 (2.75mm) dpns, or size needed to obtain gauge

Notions

Cotton waste yarn

Stitch markers

Tapestry needle

US D (3.25mm) crochet hook

Gauge

30 sts = 4" (10cm) in St st

Special Stitches

Moss Stitch (multiple of 4 sts)

RNDS 1 and 2: *K2, p2; rep from * to end of rnd.
RNDS 3 and 4: *P2, k2; rep from * to end of rnd.
Rep Rnds 1–4 for patt.

Pebble Stitch (multiple of 2 sts)

RNDS 1 and 2: K all sts.
RND 3: *K2tog; rep from * to end of rnd.
RND 4: *P1, pick up horizontal thread before next st and p into it; rep from * to end of rnd.
Rep Rnds 1–4 for patt.

Crossover Stitch (multiple of 2 sts)

RND 1: *Yo, k2, pass yo over 2 k sts; rep from * to end.
RND 2: K all sts.
RND 3: Sl 1, *yo, k2, pass yo over 2 k sts; rep from * to end.
RND 4: K to last st, sl last st.
Rep Rnds 1–4 for patt.

Striped Rib (multiple of 2 sts)

RND 1: K all sts.
RNDS 2 and 3: *K1, p1; rep from * to end of rnd.
Rep Rnds 1–3 for patt.

K1, P1 Rib (multiple of 2 sts)

RND 1: *K1, p1; rep from * to end of rnd.
Rep Rnd 1 for patt.

Knit the Toe

Using the Crochet Circular Cast On (see page 30) and Color A, CO 8 sts. Pm for beg of rnd.

Note: Round begins at side of leg, not center back.

RND 1: *KFB, k1; rep from * to end of rnd—12 sts.
RND 2: *KFB, k2; rep from * to end of rnd—16 sts.
RND 3: *KFB, k3; rep from * to end of rnd—20 sts.
RND 4: *KFB, k4; rep from * to end of rnd—24 sts.
RND 5: K all sts.
RND 6: *KFB, k5; rep from * to end of rnd—28 sts.
RND 7: K all sts.
Continue in this manner, k 1 more st after the inc and working 1 plain rnd after each inc rnd, until you have 56 sts; on this last rnd, sl the last st.

Knit the Foot

Note: See This Sock's Secret *on page 85 to learn how to create jogless joins.*

Join Color B and k 4 rnds.
Join Color C and k 8 rnds.
Join Color D and k 4 rnds.
Join Color A and k 8 rnds.
Join Color E and k 4 rnds.
Join Color B and k 4 rnds.
Join Color C and k 8 rnds.
Join Color D and k 4 rnds.
Join Color A and k 3 rnds. Do not break yarn.

Set Up for the Heel

With waste yarn, k 28 sts. Go back and pick up Color A, k the 28 sts on the waste yarn and the rem 28 sts in the rnd.

Knit the Leg

Continuing with Color A, work 4 rnds of garter st (p 1 rnd, k 1 rnd).
Join Color E and k 1 rnd. Work Rnd 2 of Moss Stitch. Work Rnds 3 and 4 of Moss Stitch, work Rnds 1–4 twice then work Rnds 1–3 again, k 1 rnd.
Join Color C and work 4 rnds of garter st.
Join Color B and work Rnds 1–4 of Pebble Stitch five times.
Join Color A and work 4 rnds of garter st.
Join Color D and work Rnds 1–4 of Crossover Stitch twice, then work Rnds 1 and 2 again.
Join Color C and work 3 rnds of garter st.

Knit the Cuff

Continuing with Color C, work 3 rnds of K1, P1 Rib.
* Work Rnds 1–3 of Striped Rib in Color E. Rep from * once with Color B, Color D and Color A.
Work the Tapestry Needle Bind Off (see page 41).

Knit the Heel

Carefully remove waste yarn from the heel sts and place 28 sts on the lower needle and 27 sts on upper needle. Divide sts onto 4 dpns starting at the seam edge. Join Color B and k one rnd, inc 1 st on the last needle. Work even in Color B for 9 more rnds.
NEXT RND (Dec Rnd): K1, k2tog at beg of Needle 1, k to end; k to last 3 sts on Needle 2, SSK, k1; k1, k2tog at beg of Needle 3, k to end; k to last 3 sts on Needle 4, SSK, k1.

Continue in this manner, dec every rnd until there are 5 sts on each needle. Sl the sts from Needle 2 onto Needle 1 and the sts from Needle 4 onto Needle 3.

Finishing
Kitchener stitch the two sets of 10 sts together (see pages 38–40).
Weave in ends. Wash and block the completed socks.
Wear in good health!

This Sock's Secret

When knitting stripes in the round like those featured in this pattern, prevent a jog in the pattern by slipping the last stitch before the color change. This forces the last stitch of the next color to drop to the row below, thus making a smooth transition.

MOSAIC SPORT SOCKS

This short sock has a heel worked with a mosaic (two-color slip stitch) pattern, while the foot features an articulated toe for easy wearing with your flip-flops.

Finished Size
Approx 7" (18cm) circumference, leg and foot length as desired.

Yarn
3 (1¾oz./50g, 186yd./203m) skeins fingering weight yarn, 2 skeins Yarn A, 1 skein Yarn B

Note: The project shown at right was made using 3 skeins of Crystal Palace Panda Wool (51% bamboo/39% wool/1% nylon, 1¾oz./50g, 186yd./203m), 2 skeins of color 9573 (A) and 1 skein of 0443 (B).

Needles
Set of 5 US 1½ (2.5mm) dpns, or one size smaller than larger needles

Set of 5 US 2 (2.75mm) dpns, or size needed to obtain gauge

1 US 1½ (2.5mm) straight needle

16" (40cm) US 1½ (2.5mm) circular needle

Notions
Cotton waste yarn

Stitch holder

Tapestry needle

Gauge
28 sts = 4" (10cm) in St st on larger needles

Mosaic Pattern

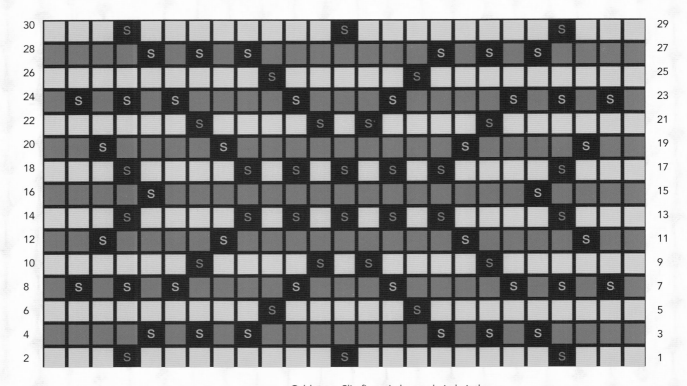

■ Color A

■ Color B

S Slip stitch using appropriate color

Odd rows: Slip first stitch as to knit; knit the last stitch.

Even rows: Slip first stitch as to purl; purl the last stitch

---

Special Stitches

Mosaic Pattern

Note: On all RS rows, slip sts pwise with yarn in back. On all WS rows, slip sts pwise with yarn in front.

ROW 1 (RS): With Color B, k3, [sl 1, k8] twice, sl 1, k3.

ROW 2 and all WS rows: K the sts that were knitted on previous row with the same color; sl all the sts that were slipped on the previous row with yarn in front.

ROW 3: With Color A, k4, [sl 1, k1] three times, k6, [sl 1, k1] three times, k4.

ROW 5: With Color B, k9, sl 1, k5, sl 1, k9.

ROW 7: With Color A, [k1, sl 1] three times, k4, sl 1, k3, sl 1, k4, [sl 1, k1] three times.

ROW 9: With Color B, k6, sl 1, k4, sl 1, k1, sl 1, k4, sl 1, k6.

ROW 11: With Color A, k2, sl 1, k4, sl 1, k9, sl 1, k4, sl 1, k2.

ROW 13: With Color B, k3, sl 1, k4, [sl 1, k1] four times, sl 1, k4, sl 1, k3.

ROW 15: With Color A, k4, sl 1, k15, sl 1, k4.

ROW 17: With Color B, rep Row 13.

ROW 19: With Color A, rep Row 11.

ROW 21: With Color B, rep Row 9.

ROW 23: With Color A, rep Row 7.

ROW 25: With Color B, rep Row 5.

ROW 27: With Color A, rep Row 3.

ROW 29: With Color B, rep Row 1.

Knit the Leg

Using the Invisible Provisional Cast On (see page 29), a straight needle and Color A, CO 54 sts. Divide evenly onto 4 smaller needles and join into a round taking care not to twist the sts.

Note: Round begins at side of leg, not center back.

Work St st for 12 rnds, approx 1" (3cm), slipping the last st of the last rnd.

P 1 rnd. This creates the turning ridge that will become the top of the sock.

K 12 rnds.

Place provisional CO sts onto circular needle, remove waste yarn, and fold along the turning ridge.

To join the facing to the inside of the Leg, k 1 st on dpns tog with 1 provisional CO st from circular needle. Change to larger dpns and k 8 rnds.

Divide for the Heel

K the first 27 sts onto one needle for the Heel Flap. Leave rem 27 sts on hold for the Instep. Turn and p 1 WS row on the 27 heel sts.

Knit the Heel Flap

Join Color B.

ROW 1: Sl 1 kwise, work Row 1 of Mosaic Pattern over next 25 sts, k1.

ROW 2: Sl 1 pwise, work Row 1 of Mosaic Pattern over next 25 sts, p1.

Maintaining edge sts as est, work through Row 30 of Mosaic Pattern.

Cut Color B, leaving a tail to weave in later. With Color A, k 1 row, p 1 row, sl the first st of each row.

Turn the Heel

ROW 1 (RS): Sl 1 kwise, k15, SSK, k1, turn.

ROW 2 (WS): Sl 1 pwise, p6, p2tog, p1, turn.

ROW 3: Sl 1 pwise, k7, SSK, k1, turn.

ROW 4: Sl 1 pwise, p8, p2tog, p1, turn.

Continue in this manner, working 1 more st before dec each row, until 17 sts rem. K 1 RS row, sl the first and last sts of this row (see *This Sock's Secret* on page 77).

Knit the Gussets

Note: Pick up and k through both loops of chain sts.

With the same needle that holds the heel sts, pick up and k 16 chain sts along one side of the Heel Flap. With a new needle, pick up last chain st and SSK this st tog with the first instep st. Work 25 instep sts. K the last instep st tog with the first chain st on other side of the Heel Flap. With a new needle, pick up and k 16 chain sts along other side of the Heel Flap, then k 9 heel sts onto same needle—76 sts.

Note: Round now begins at the center back.

Shape the Gussets

RND 1: K to last 2 sts on Needle 1, k2tog; k instep sts; SSK at the beg of Needle 4, k to end.

RND 2: K all sts.

Rep Rnds 1–2 until 54 sts rem.

Knit the Foot

Continue in St st until the Foot measures 7" (18cm) from back of the Heel or 1¾" (4cm) less than desired finished length.

Right Sock

Knit the Toes

K32. Place next 16 sts on holder for the Big Toe. CO 6 sts using the Purl Cable Cast On (see *This Sock's Secret* on page 91), then k the last 6 sts of the rnd—44 sts. Rearrange sts so there are 17 sts on Needle 1, 17 sts on Needle 2, and 10 sts on Needle 3. Needle 3 should hold the 6 CO sts and 2 sts on each side of these 6 sts.

Shape the Toe

K 3 rnds.

RND 1: K to last three sts on Needle 1, k2tog, k1; on Needle 2, k1, SSK, k to end; on Needle 3, k2tog, k6, SSK—40 sts.

RNDs 2: K to last three sts on Needle 1, k2tog, k1; on Needle 2, k1, SSK, k to end; on Needle 3, k all sts—38 sts.

RNDS 3 and 4: K all sts.

RNDs 5 and 6: Rep Rnd 2.

RNDS 7–9: K all sts.

RND 10: Rep Rnd 2.

RND 11: K to last three sts on Needle 1, k2tog, k1; on Needle 2, k1, SSK, k to end; on Needle 3, SSK, k4, k2tog—28 sts.

RND 12: Rep Rnd 2.

RNDS 13–15: K all sts.

RNDs 16 and 17: Rep Rnd 2.

RNDS 18–20: K all sts.

Sl 3 sts from Needle 3 onto Needle 1 and 3 sts from Needle 3 onto Needle 2. Kitchener stitch the two sets of 11 sts together (see pages 38–40).

Knit the Big Toe

Place 8 held sts onto Needle 1 and 8 held sts onto Needle 2. With Needle 3, pick up and k the 6 CO sts—22 sts. Join into a round and work in St st for 14 rnds.

Shape the Big Toe

RND 1: On Needles 1 and 2, k all sts; SSK, k2, k2tog on Needle 3—20 sts.
RNDS 2 and 3: K all sts.
RND 4: On Needle 1, k3, k2tog, k3; on Needle 2, k3, k2tog, k3; on Needle 3, k4—18 sts.
RNDS 5 and 6: K all sts.
RND 7: On Needle 1, k2tog, k3, k2tog; on Needle 2, k2tog, k3, k2tog; on Needle 3, k4—14 sts.
RND 8: K all sts.
RND 9: *K2tog; rep from * to end of rnd—7 sts.
Thread tail onto tapestry needle and run through rem 7 sts twice. Pull up snug and fasten off.

Left Sock

Knit the Toes

K5, place next 16 sts on hold for the Big Toe, CO 6 sts using the Purl Cable Cast On (see *This Sock's Secret*, page 91), k to end of rnd—44 sts. Rearrange sts so there are 10 sts on Needle 1, 17 sts on Needle 2 and 17 sts on Needle 3. Needle 1 should hold the 6 CO sts and 2 sts on each side of these 6 sts.

Shape the Toe

K 3 rnds.
RND 1: On Needle 1, k2tog, k6, SSK; k to last three sts on Needle 2, k2tog, k1; on Needle 3, k1, SSK, k to end—40 sts.
RND 2: On Needle 1, k all sts; k to last three sts on Needle 2, k2tog, k1; on Needle 3, k1, SSK, k to end—38 sts.
RNDS 3 and 4: K all sts.
RNDS 5 and 6: Rep Rnd 2.
RNDS 7–9: K all sts.
RND 10: Rep Rnd 2.
RND 11: On Needle 1, SSK, k4, k2tog; k to last three sts on Needle 2, k2tog, k1; on Needle 3, k1, SSK, k to end—28 sts.
RND 12: Rep Rnd 2.
RNDS 13–15: K all sts.
RND 16 and 17: Rep Rnd 2.
RNDS 18–20: K all sts.
Sl 3 sts from Needle 1 onto Needle 3 and 3 sts from Needle 1 onto Needle 2.
Kitchener stitch the two sets of 11 sts together (see pages 38–40).

Knit the Big Toe

Work same as for Right Sock.

Shape the Big Toe

Work same as for Right Sock.

Finishing

Weave in ends. Wash and block the completed socks. Wear in good health!

This Sock's Secret

A Purl Cable Cast On is used in this sock to add extra stitches to existing ones already on the needle. It is done purlwise because the wrong side of the work is facing you at that point in the construction.

With wrong side facing, place the right needle from back to front between the last two stitches on the left needle. Yarn over as if to purl, then draw the loop through. Place the new stitch on the left needle. Repeat for the required number of stitches.

FAIR ISLE SOCKS

My sock collection would not be complete without a Fair Isle pattern. The various motifs are separated by solid rows and peeries, the name given to the smallest of the designs. Patterns abound, and the only plain areas are on the toe and the bottom of the heel.

Finished Size
Approx 8" (20cm) leg circumference and 7" (18cm) foot circumference, leg and foot length as desired.

Yarn
2 (1¾oz./50g, 231yd./211m) skeins fingering weight yarn, 1 each of 2 colors (MC and CC)

Note: The project shown at right was made using 2 skeins of KnitPicks Essential Sock Yarn (75% superwash wool/25% nylon, 1¾oz./50g, 231yd./211m), 1 each of colors 23692 (MC) and 23701 (CC).

Needles
Set of 5 US 2 (2.75mm) dpns, or one size smaller than larger needles

Set of 5 US 3 (3.25mm) dpns, or size needed to obtain gauge

US 3 (3.25mm) straight needles

Notions
Stitch markers

Tapestry needle

Gauge
32 sts = 4" (10cm) in St st on larger needles

Fair Isle Pattern

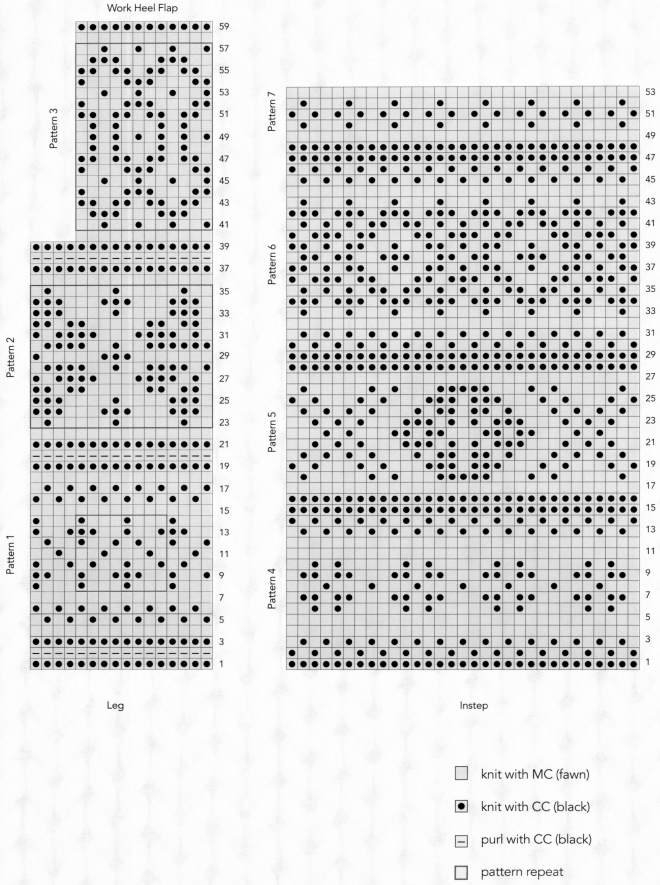

Work Heel Flap

Pattern 3

Pattern 2

Pattern 1

Leg

Pattern 7

Pattern 6

Pattern 5

Pattern 4

Instep

☐ knit with MC (fawn)

⬤ knit with CC (black)

⊟ purl with CC (black)

☐ pattern repeat

Both Socks

Knit the Cuff

Using the Long-Tail Cast On (see page 25), CC and a straight needle, CO 64 sts. Turn and k 1 row. Distribute sts evenly onto 4 smaller needles and join into a round, taking care not to twist the sts. The purl side of the CO is facing outward. Pm for beg of rnd.

Note: Round begins at side of leg, not center back.

RND 1: K all sts.
RND 2: *K2 with CC, k2 with MC; rep from * to end of rnd.
RND 3: *K2 with CC, p2 with MC; rep from * to end of rnd.
Rep Rnd 3 until cuff measures 2" (5cm) from beg.

Knit the Leg

Change to larger dpns. Work Leg chart through Rnd 39.
RND 40: Dec 1 st on each needle by k2tog—60 sts rem. Continue chart through Pattern 3.
Cut MC. K1 rnd with CC.

Right Sock

Divide for the Heel

The Heel is worked on Needles 1 and 2 over 29 sts. With CC, k 15 sts on Needle 1 and 14 sts on Needle 2 onto the same needle. Slide rem st on Needle 2 onto Needle 3. There are 16 sts on Needle 3 and 15 sts on Needle 4 for the Instep—31 sts. Join MC to heel sts.

Knit the Heel Flap

SET-UP ROW (WS): Sl 1 kwise, *p1 with CC, p1 with MC; rep from * to end.
ROW 1 (RS): Sl 1 kwise, *k1 with MC, k1 with CC; rep from * to end.
ROW 2: Sl 1 kwise, *p1 with CC, p1 with MC; rep from * to end.
Rep Rows 1–2 nine more times, then Row 1 once more. You now have 11 chain sts along each side of the Heel Flap. Cut MC. With CC, p1 WS row.

Turn the Heel

ROW 1 (RS): K17, SSK, k1, turn.
ROW 2 (WS): Sl 1 pwise, p6, p2tog, p1, turn.
ROW 3: Sl 1 kwise, k7, SSK, k1, turn.
ROW 4: Sl 1 pwise, p8, p2tog, p1, turn.
Continue in this manner, working 1 more st before the dec on each row, until 17 sts rem. K 1 RS row, sl the first and last sts of this row (see *This Sock's Secret* on page 77).

Knit the Gussets

Note: Pick up and k through both loops of chain sts.

With a new needle, pick up and k 11 chain sts along one side of the Heel Flap and 1 st in the corner before instep sts; with a new needle, work the 31 instep sts foll Rnd 1 of Instep chart; with a new needle, pick up and k 1 st in the corner and 11 chain sts along other side of the Heel Flap—72 sts. Cut CC.
Join MC and CC at right seam line.

Shape the Gussets

RND 1: K2tog at beg of Needle 1; work rem gusset sts on Needle 1, all heel sts on Needle 2, and to last 2 sts on Needle 3 foll Rnd 2 of Sole chart; SSK last 2 sts on Needle 3; work instep sts foll Rnd 2 of instep chart on Needle 4.
RND 2: Work even in patt as given on charts.
Rep Rnds 1–2 until 60 sts rem.

Left Sock

Divide for the Heel

The Heel is worked on Needles 3 and 4 over 29 sts. With CC, k 15 sts on Needle 1 and 15 sts on Needle 2 and 1 st from Needle 3 onto the same needle for the Instep—31 sts. With CC, k 14 sts on Needle 3 and 15 sts on Needle 4 onto the same needle for the Heel—29 sts. Join MC.

Knit the Heel Flap

Work same as for Right Sock.

Turn the Heel

Work same as for Right Sock.

Knit the Gussets

Note: Pick up and k through both loops of chain sts.

With a new needle, pick up and k 11 chain sts along one side of the Heel Flap and 1 st in the corner before instep sts; with a new needle, work the 31 instep sts foll Rnd 1 of the Instep chart; with a new needle, pick up and k 1 st in the corner and 11 chain sts along other side of the Heel Flap—72 sts. Cut CC.
Join MC and CC at left seam line.

Fair Isle Pattern Continued

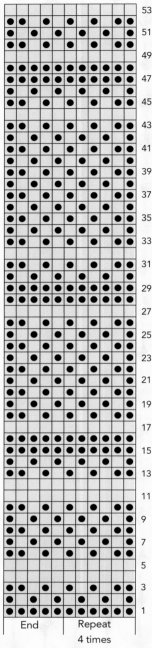

End | Repeat 4 times

Sole

Symbol Key

☐ knit with MC (fawn)

⦿ knit with CC (black)

Shape the Gussets
RND 1: Work instep sts foll Rnd 2 of the Instep chart on Needle 1; k2tog at beg of Needle 2; work rem gusset sts on Needle 2, all heel sts on Needle 3, and to last 2 sts on Needle 4 according to Rnd 2 of Sole chart; SSK last 2 sts on Needle 4.
RND 2: Work even in patt as given on charts.
Rep Rnds 1–2 until 60 sts rem.

Both Socks

Knit the Foot
Continue working foll charts until the Foot measures 7½" (19cm) from back of Heel or 2" (5cm) less than desired finished measurement. Cut MC.

Note: For Right Sock only, k 29 sole sts with CC. Round now begins at left seamline.

Shape the Toe
Redistribute sts, if necessary, so you have the first 16 instep sts on Needle 1, the last 15 instep sts on Needle 2, the first 15 sole sts on Needle 3 and the last 14 sole sts on Needle 4.
RND 1: K1, k2tog at beg of Needle 1; k to last 3 sts on Needle 2, SSK, k1; k2tog at beg of Needle 3, k to end; k to last 2 sts on Needle 4, SSK.
RND 2: K all sts.
Rep Rnds 1–2 until 16 sts rem. Sl sts from Needle 1 to Needle 2 and sts from Needle 3 to Needle 4. Sl 1 st from each end of Needle 2 to Needle 4.

Finishing
Kitchener stitch the two sets of 8 sts together (see page 38–40).
Weave in ends. Wash and block the completed socks. Wear in good health!

This Sock's Secret

The method used to work the first five rows of these socks prevents the main color from showing over the top of the rib. The first three rows are similar to the decorative rows between leg patterns.

EMBROIDERED TRELLIS SOCKS

This sock features seed stitch at the cuff and in columns down the leg. The Stockinette stitch panels between the seed stitch columns form a trellis for some lovely flower embroidery. Embroider the flowers with your favorite colors of wool tapestry yarn, silk or any other yarn or thread that strikes your fancy.

Finished Size
Approx 7" (18cm) circumference, leg and foot length as desired.

Yarn
1 (3½oz./100g, 225yd./206m) skein sport weight yarn

Note: The project shown at right was made using 1 skein of Louet Gems (100% merino wool, 3½oz./100g, 225yd./206m), color 50.

Needles
Set of 5 US 2 (2.75mm) dpns, or two sizes smaller than larger needles

Set of 5 US 4 (3.5mm) dpns, or size needed to obtain gauge

1 US 5 (3.75mm) straight needle

Notions
Tapestry needle

Yarn or thread for embroidery

Gauge
32 sts = 4" (10cm) in St st on larger needles

Knit the Leg

Using the Patterned Cast On (see page 27) and a straight needle, CO 49 sts in K1, P1 rib. Distribute sts evenly onto 4 larger needles. Join into a round taking care not to twist the sts.

Note: Round begins at side of leg, not center back.

RND 1: *K1, p1; rep from * to last st, k1.
RND 2: *P1, k1; rep from * to last st, p1.
Rep Rnds 1–2 five more times.
SET-UP RND: K2, *seed st 3 sts as est (k into p sts and p into k sts), k1, KFB, k1; rep from * to last 5 sts, seed st 3 sts as est, k2—56 sts.
NEXT RND: K2, *seed st 3 sts as est, k4; rep from * to last 5 sts, seed st 3 sts as est, k2.
Rep last rnd until piece measures 7" (18cm) from beg, or desired length to top of the Heel.
NEXT RND: K2, [seed st 3 sts as est, k2, k2tog] three times, seed st 3 sts as est, k4, [seed st 3 sts as est, k2, k2tog] three times, seed st 3 sts as est, k2—50 sts.

Divide for the Heel

ROW 1 (RS): Sl 1 pwise, seed st 23 sts as est, k1, turn. Leave rem 25 sts on hold for the Instep.
ROW 2 (WS): Sl 1 pwise, seed st 24 sts as est.
Rep Rows 1–2 over 25 heel sts eleven more times. You now have 12 chain sts along each side of the Heel Flap.

Turn the Heel

ROW 1 (RS): Seed st 15 sts as est, SSK, k1, turn.
ROW 2 (WS): P7, p2tog, p1, turn.
ROW 3: K8, SSK, k1, turn.
ROW 4: P9, p2tog, SSK, p1, turn.
Continue in this manner, working 1 more st before the dec in each row, until 15 heel sts rem. K 1 RS row, sl the first and last sts of this row (see *This Sock's Secret* on page 77).

Knit the Gussets

Note: Pick up and k through both loops of chain sts.

With the same needle that holds the heel sts, pick up and k 12 chain sts along one side of the Heel Flap. K 25 instep sts. With a new needle, pick up and k 12 chain sts along other side of the Heel Flap, then k 8 heel sts onto the same needle—64 sts.
RND 1: K to last 2 sts on Needle 1, k2tog; k instep sts on Needles 2 and 3; SSK at beg of Needle 4, k to end.
RND 2: K all sts.
Rep Rnds 1–2 until 50 sts rem.

Knit the Foot

Continue even in St st until the Foot measures 7" (18cm) from back of the Heel or 1½" (4cm) less than desired finished length.

Shape the Toe

RND 1: K1, *k5, k2tog; rep from * to end of rnd—43 sts.
RNDS 2 and 3: K all sts.
RND 4: K1, *k2tog, k4; rep from * to end of rnd—36 sts.
RNDS 5 and 6: K all sts.
RND 7: K1, *k2tog, k3; rep from * to end of rnd—29 sts.
RNDS 8 and 9: K all sts.
RND 10: K1, *k2tog, k2; rep from * to end of rnd—22 sts.
RNDS 11 and 12: K all sts.
RND 13: K1, *k2tog, k1; rep from * to end of rnd—15 sts.
RNDS 14 and 15: K all sts.
RND 16: *K2tog; rep from * to last st, k1 of rnd—8 sts.

Finishing

Break yarn, leaving a 10" (25cm) tail. Thread the tail onto the tapestry needle and draw it through the rem sts. Pull up snug and fasten off.
Embroider flowers using chain stitch, lazy daisies and French knots.
Weave in ends. Wash and block the completed socks. Wear in good health!

This Sock's Secret

To ensure evenly spaced embroidery, I use embroidery thread to mark the sock before I stitch the flowers. The blue thread in the photo above is used to count the number of rows from the bottom of the cuff to the beginning of the heel (fifty four in this sample). The green diagonal lines are the trellis base.

To create the trellis base, thread a tapestry needle with green yarn. Secure the yarn at the top right side of a four-stitch Stockinette panel, count down six rows on the left side of the same panel, then insert the needle under the sixth row and come out between the second and third rows. Count down twelve rows on the right side of the same panel, insert the needle under the twelfth row and come out between the seventh and eight rows. Continue in this manner, alternating threads on each side of the Stockinette panel until the heel is reached.

THRUMMED HOUSE SOCKS

Putting these socks on is like stepping into a down comforter! Tufts of roving are knitted in to make a contrasting stitch on the outside and a warm and fluffy piece of insulation on the inside.

Finished Size
Approx 9" (23cm) circumference, leg and foot length as desired.

Yarn
2 (3½oz./100g, 132yd./120m) skeins heavy worsted weight yarn (A)

Note: The project shown at right was made using 2 skeins of Cascade Yarns Pastaza (50% llama/50% wool, 3½oz./100g, 132yd./120m), color 031.

Needles
Set of 5 US 7 (4.5mm) dpns, or two sizes smaller than larger needles

Set of 5 US 9 (5.5mm) dpns, or size needed to obtain gauge

1 US 9 (5.5mm) straight needle

Notions
1 oz. (28g) merino wool roving (B)

Tapestry needle

Waste yarn

Gauge
16 sts = 4" (10cm) in St st on larger needles

Special Stitches

Cable Rib (multiple of 4 sts)

RNDS 1, 2, and 4: With A, *k3, p1; rep from * to end of rnd.
RND 3: *K the third st on the needle and lift it over the first 2 sts, k the 2 sts on the needle, p1; rep from * to end of rnd.
Rep Rnds 1–4 for patt.

Thrummed Pattern (multiple of 4 sts)

RND 1: With A, k all sts.
RND 2: K1 with A, *k1 tbl with B, k3 with A; rep from * to last 3 sts, k1 tbl with B, k2 with A.
RND 3: With A, k1, *k1 tbl, k3; rep from * to last 3 sts, k1 tbl, k2.
RND 4: With A, k all sts.
RND 5: K3 with A, * k1 tbl with B, k3 with A; rep from * to last st, k1 tbl with B.
RND 6: With A, k3, *k1 tbl, k3; rep from * to last st, k1 tbl.
Rep Rnds 1–6 for patt.

Prepare Roving

Cut B into 6" (15cm) lengths and lightly twist each length. Hold two ends together and allow roving to twist onto itself. Fold in half.

Knit the Leg

Using Patterned Cast On (see page 27), a straight needle and Color A, CO 40 sts in K3, P1 rib. Distribute evenly onto 4 larger needless and join into a round taking care not to twist the sts.

Note: Round begins at side of leg, not center back.

Change to smaller needles and work Cable Rib for 2½" (6cm) ending on Rnd 4.
Change to larger dpns and work three reps of Thrummed Pattern ending on Rnd 6.

Set Up for the Heel

With waste yarn, k 20 sts. Go back and pick up A, k the 20 sts on the waste yarn and the rem 20 sts in the rnd.

Knit the Foot

With A and B, work Rnds 2–6 of Thrummed Pattern. Continue working Thrummed Pattern until Foot measures approx 6" (15cm) from waste yarn or 2" (5cm) less than desired finished length.

Shape the Toe

Note: Continue the Thrummed Pattern through end of toe shaping.

RND 1: K1, k2tog, k to end of Needle 1; k to last 3 sts of Needle 2, SSK, k1; k1, k2tog at beg of Needle 3, k to end; k to last 3 sts on Needle 4, SSK, k1.
RND 2: Work even in patt.
Rep Rnds 1–2 until 4 sts rem on each needle.
K 4 sts from Needle 1 onto Needle 2. Sl 4 sts from Needle 3 onto Needle 4.
Kitchener stitch the two sets of 8 sts together (see pages 38–40).

Shape the Heel

Carefully remove waste yarn from the heel sts and place 20 sts on the lower needle and 19 sts on upper needle. Divide sts onto 4 dpns starting at the seam edge. Join A and k 1 rnd, inc 1 st on the last needle. Work even in A for 6 more rnds.
DEC RND: K2tog at beg of Needle 1, k to end; k to last 2 sts on Needle 2, SSK; k2tog at beg of Needle 3, k to end; k to last 2 sts on Needle 4, SSK.
Continue in this manner, dec on every rnd until there are 4 sts on each needle. Sl the sts from Needle 2 onto Needle 1 and the sts from Needle 4 onto Needle 3.

Finishing

Kitchener stitch the two sets of 8 sts together (see pages 38–40).
Weave in ends. Wash and block the completed socks.
Wear in good health!

This Sock's Secret

When knitting a stitch with roving the way this pattern calls for, insert the needle into the back of the stitch, place a piece of roving over the needle and complete the stitch. When you come to this stitch on the next round, knit into the back to lock the stitch in place.

Basic Knitting Information

Knitting Needle Conversions

diameter (mm)	US size	suggested yarn weight
2	0	Lace Weight
2.25	1	Lace and Fingering Weight
2.5	1½	Lace and Fingering Weight
2.75	2	Lace and Fingering Weight
3	2½	Lace and Fingering Weight
3.25	3	Fingering and Sport Weight
3.5	4	Fingering and Sport Weight
3.75	5	DK and Sport Weight
4	6	DK, Sport and Aran/Worsted Weight
4.5	7	Aran/Worsted Worsted
5	8	Aran/Worsted and Heavy Worsted
5.5	9	Aran/Worsted, Heavy Worsted and Chunky/Bulky
6	10	Chunky/Bulky
6.5	10½	Chunky/Bulky and Super Bulky
8	11	Chunky/Bulky and Super Bulky
9	13	Super Bulky
10	15	Super Bulky
12.75	17	Super Bulky
15	19	Super Bulky
20	36	Super Bulky

Standard Knitting Abbreviations

approx	approximately
beg	begin, beginning
CC	contrast color
cn	cable needle
CO	cast on
dec	decrease
dpn(s)	double-pointed needle(s)
est	established
foll	following
inc	increase
k	knit
KFB	knit 1 front and back
k2tog	knit 2 together
kwise	knitwise, as if to knit
MC	main color
p	purl
(in) patt	(in) pattern
p2sso	pass 2 slipped stitches over
p2tog	purl 2 together
pm	place marker
psso	pass slipped stitch over
pwise	purlwise
rem	remaining
rnd	round
RS	right side
rep	repeat
SKP	slip 1, knit 1, pass slipped stitch over
sl	slip
SSK	slip, slip, knit
st(s)	stitch(es)
St st	Stockinette stitch
tbl	through back loop
tog	together
WS	wrong side
yo	yarn over

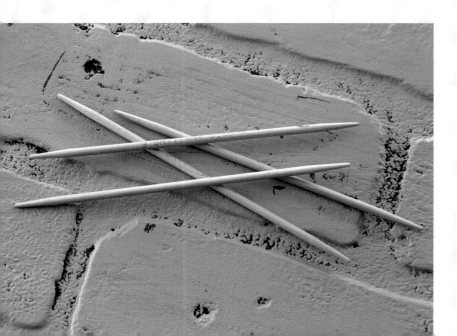

Yarn Weight Guidelines

Since the names given to different weights of yarn can vary widely depending on the country of origin or the yarn manufacturer's preference, the Craft Yarn Council of America has put together a standard yarn weight system to impose a bit of order on the sometimes unruly yarn labels. Look for a picture of a skein of yarn with a number 0–6 on most kinds of yarn to figure out its "official" weight. Gauge is given over 4" (10cm) of Stockinette stitch. The information in the chart below is taken from www.yarnstandards.com.

	SUPER BULKY (6)	BULKY (5)	MEDIUM (4)	LIGHT (3)	FINE (2)	SUPERFINE (1)	LACE (0)
TYPE	6	5	4	3	2	1	0
	bulky, roving	chunky, craft, rug	worsted, afgan, aran	DK, light, worsted	sport, baby	sock, fingering, baby	fingering, 10-count crochet thread
KNIT GAUGE RANGE	6-11 sts	12-15 sts	16-20 sts	21-24 sts	23-26 sts	27-32 sts	33-40 sts
RECOMMENDED NEEDLE IN U.S. SIZE RANGE	11 and larger	9 to 11	7 to 9	5 to 7	3 to 5	1 to 3	000 to 1

Substituting Yarns

If you substitute yarn, be sure to select a yarn of the same weight as the yarn recommended for the project. Even after checking that the recommended gauge on the yarn you plan to substitute is the same as for the yarn listed in the pattern, knit a swatch to ensure that the yarn and needles you are using will produce the correct gauge.

Resources

As previously mentioned, the knitting market is rife with suppliers of top quality yarns, needles and other supplies. The following list includes the companies whose needles, yarns and accessories I used while knitting and writing this book, with thanks for their support.

Brittany Birch Knitting Needles & Crochet Hooks
Phone: 707-877-1881
www.brittanyneedles.com
Knitting needles

Cascade Yarns, Inc.
Phone: 206-574-0440
www.cascadeyarns.com
Yarn

Cherry Tree Hill Yarn
Phone: 802-525-3311
www.cherryyarn.com
Yarn

Crystal Palace Yarns
Phone: 510-237-9988
www.crystalpalaceyarns.com
Yarn, Point protectors, Yarn cutters

Knit Picks
Phone: 800-574-1323
www.knitpicks.com
Nickel-plated needles, Yarn

Louet North America
Phone: 800-897-6444
www.louet.com
Yarn

Mountain Colors, Inc.
Phone: 406-961-1900
www.mountaincolors.com
Yarn

Nordic Fiber Arts
Phone: 603-868-1196
www.nordicfiberarts.com
Yarn

Norwegian Spirit, Inc.
Phone: 866-347-0809
www.spirit-norway.com
Yarn

Rowan
Phone: 800-445-9276
www.knitrowan.com
Yarn

Schaefer Yarn Company
Phone: 607-532-9452
www.schaeferyarn.com
Yarn

Bibliography

Lucky for us, there have been hundreds of books published that provide loads of information about the history of knitting, general and specific knitting techniques, and designs for everything from socks to sweaters. These are the books I referred to while knitting and writing this book.

Bush, Nancy. *Folk Socks: The History and Techniques of Handknitted Footwear.* Loveland, CO: Interweave Press, 1994.

Don, Sarah. *Fair Isle Knitting.* New York: St Martin's Press, 1979.

Hamilton Hill, Margot and Peter Bucknell. *The Evolution of Fashion.* New York: Drama Book Specialists, 1968.

Laver, James. *The Concise History of Costume and Fashion.* New York: Charles Scribner's Sons, 1969.

Macdonald, Ann L. *No Idle Hands: The Social History of American Knitting.* New York: Ballantine Books, 1990.

Rutt, Richard. *A History of Hand Knitting.* Loveland, CO: Interweave Press, 1989.

Smith, Mary and Maggie Twatt. *A Shetland Pattern Book.* The Shetland Times, Ltd. 1979.

Starmore, Alice. *Fair Isle Knitting.* Connecticut: The Taunton Press, 1988.

Thomas, Mary. *Mary Thomas's Knitting Book.* New York: Dover Publications, 1972.

Index